A NEW VISION
OF SPYCRAFT

Or Necessary Notations On Espionage

DANIELE-HADI IRANDOOST

PREFACE & EDITED BY DAVID WILLIAM PARRY

BY THE SAME AUTHOR

On the Philosophy of Education:
Towards an Anthroposophical View

978-0-6456700-6-6

A New Vision of Spycraft:
Or Necessary Notations On Espionage
Daniele-Hadi Irandoost
Preface and edited by David William Parry

MANTICORE PRESS
WWW.MANTICORE.PRESS

For my partner

DWP

CONTENTS

CLOAKS & INTRODUCTORY DAGGERS BY DAVID WILLIAM
PARRY   9

PART I
The Need to Watch Our Watchers

CHAPTER I

THE OPERATION OF INTELLIGENCE CONSIDERED AS A
SUBJECT OF POLITICAL INSTITUTIONS IN SOCIETIES   15

Spirit of Intelligence   18
The Intelligence Cycle   19
Counterintelligence   20
Covert Action   2_
Strategic Deception   22
Enquiry Concerning Intelligence   24

CHAPTER II

OF THE DIFFERENCE OF MORALS:
CAN INTELLIGENCE EVER BE ETHICALLY SOUND?   27

Right to Torture Whence Derived   29
Good and Evil Apparent   31
The Third Normative Framework, Just Intelligence Theory 34
Purgatory for the Spook, Howsoever Understood   37

CHAPTER III

AN INTERDISCIPLINARY INVESTIGATION:
THE CIVILIZING PROCESS AND THE STUDY OF INTELLIGENCE   41

Intelligence and Process Sociology, Considered Together   43
Idealist Propositions: Their Mixed Modes and Relations   47
Civilized Intelligence and its Distinct Imperfections   52
Of the Improvement of Eliasian Studies, or Vice Versa   56

CHAPTER IV

THE EFFECT WHICH AN HETEROGENOUS ASSOCIATION OF
TECHNOLOGICAL DEVELOPMENTS AND PRACTICES, SUCH AS
CYBERCRIME, HAS UPON NATIONAL AND INTERNATIONAL LAW 59

The Involved Opinions of Law for Cyberspace Considered   60
The Same Topic Comprehensively Considered   63
*Animadversions on the Degradation of National
Cybersecurity*   65
Concluding Reflections on the Modesty of Cyber Law   68

PART II

Overseeing Those With Oversight

INTRODUCTORY WORDS AND PLAN OF THE WORK   73

CHAPTER V

OF INTELLIGENCE OVERSIGHT AND EFFECTIVENESS,
WITH THEIR DIFFERENCE   79

Drawbacks of Oversight   81
Analysis of the Preceding Drawbacks   84
The Proper Objects of Oversight   88
The Future of Oversight, and Differences of Bearing   95

CHAPTER VI

REFLECTIONS ON THE OVERSIGHT OF THE
INTELLIGENCE AND SECURITY COMMITTEE 99

How to Judge the Proper Influence of the ISC 101
The Women of the UK Intelligence Community 102
Draft Investigatory Powers Bill 105
Transparency 107
The Sense of Accessibility and Inaccessibility 112

CHAPTER VII

THOUGHTS ON THE STRUCTURAL STRENGTHS AND WEAKNESSES
OF THE INTELLIGENCE AND SECURITY COMMITTEE 115

The Propriety of Membership 117
Reporting 121
Mandate 122
Complete Access to Information 125
Political Will 128
Recapitulation of the Chapter 130

CONCLUDING REMARKS FOR PART II 133

APPENDIX

CLASSICAL AND SOCIAL LIBERALS ON THE
APPROPRIATE RANGE OF STATE ACTIVITIES 139

Why Minimal Government is Necessary 140
Of the Origin of Social Liberalism 141
Limitations of Classical Liberalism 143
Of Skepticism with Regard to Social Liberalism 144
Conclusion of this Appendix 145

AUTHOR'S AFTERWORD   149

BIBLIOGRAPHY   153

ACKNOWLEDGEMENTS   169

SOURCE NOTES   171

CLOAKS

&

INTRODUCTORY DAGGERS

S pycraft and the world of espionage have always been very far from me. Indeed, the lurid techniques employed by Machiavellian state officials in their desperate need to keep a toxic and porcine ruling elite in position has invariably filled me with little apart from despair. A type of cultural depression partially alleviated by a chance remark made by my dear friend, Richard Rudgley, many years ago when he said spying and occultism had always been historically associated. An off-the-cuff observation that intrigued me enough to allude to this prescient intuition in a talk I myself gave to the Free Speech Club in its heyday, as well as Eurasian Creative Guild some time later. Altogether resulting, in an ever-advancing cacophony of absurdities since that long-ago period.

Anyway, looking back, I recall being mindful on both occasions of early almost nonsensical alliterative renditions of 'I am a Mole and I Live in a Hole' by the 1950s Anglo-Jamaican group, The Southlanders. A song forever identified with them, even though if memory serves me correctly, their biggest commercial hit was actually the 1958 cover version of 'Alone.' Yet, digressions notwithstanding, 'I am a Mole and I Live in a Hole' is a modest enough jingle which held little personal significance for me until I was told (by certain friends of mine after these meetings) some people had started saying I was that very mole. Overall, not enough 'nasty' things had been written about me in the press, whereas I openly still had cherished colleagues across the political spectrum: each indirectly implying, of course, I was either collecting information for some clandestine government agency, or infiltrating these gatherings for unspecified, but obviously provocative, purposes. Well, from my side I confess to openly speaking about Christian anarchism across Europe since 1996 to anyone kind enough to invite me as a guest speaker, while my public protests along these lines had occasionally been reported to the papers. All in all, a predestined eventuality leading to false accusations by goose-stepping 'liberals' active on social media without any real recourse to the records. All making me think, as a threadbare Old Catholic priest, it would never hurt these self-appointed pundits to check their sources, whereas any MI5 annuity would be more than welcome amid my endlessly strained finances. Either way, the misinformation and social subterfuge surrounding such fields of endeavor remain distant, albeit telling, memories.

In which case, I can heartily recommend Daniele-Hadi Irandoost's book on spying, evocatively entitled *A New Vision of Spycraft: Or Necessary Notations on Espionage*, to anyone and everyone interested in the mechanics of espionage, so-called government oversight of intelligence garnering agencies and politically motivated gossip, alongside unexpected institutional links to the deepest and darkest type of occultism. After all, I am not a mole who lives in a hole, let me repeat I am not a mole who lives in a hole, even though I am fully aware that these shadowy spheres can blight anyone's reputation, whilst their own motives must never be taken at face value. As such, this volume is unarguably a must-read!

DAVID WILLIAM PARRY
Isle of Bute
July, 2023

PART I

THE NEED TO WATCH OUR WATCHERS

CHAPTER I

The word *intelligence* is a term extremely vague in its signification. It is generally admitted that its whole history may be traced to its remotest source found among the ancient volumes if the Jewish Old Testament, *The Art of War* by Sun Tzu, and the *Arthashastra* were added to the list.[1] Afterward, this general term was successively repeated among the inhabitants of Ancient Greece and Rome, as well as during the Islamic Golden Age and the Renaissance of Europe. The histories here mentioned on the conduct of intelligence lead the mind to a very interesting subject: divination and astrology as the instruments of their purposes. If we compare the case of diviners and the adherents of the rationalism, which burst into explosion at the age of reason, some extraordinary talents will be brought to our minds. There could not perhaps be a better example than that of John Dee, the English mathematician, astronomer, astrologer, occult philosopher, and Queen Elizabeth I's tutor-adviser, who engaged in a careful development of close relations with the Virgin Queen's spymaster, Francis Walsingham. Indeed, the whole period of his existence was devoted to the study of alchemy and Hermeticism; he invented with indefatigable care the plan for the imperial expansion of England, which he most properly termed, the British Empire. As such, Dee corresponded between the boundless catalog of science and the chilling system of ancient magical inheritances, just as the former was gaining ground, upon which he trained many who advanced in England's voyage of discovery of every other quarter of the globe. In any case, the connection between intelligence and occultism or the paranormal is affirmable and will be found to surface from time to time. Aleister Crowley is the best modern example. Crowley founded a new religious movement (which is usually called Thelema) and frequently had the opportunity of seeing the most intriguing types of people who were involved in all the mischiefs of espionage at the time: in this instance, I can think of Maxwell Knight, Ian Fleming, Dennis Wheatley, and Roald Dahl;[1] whereas he, as Richard B. Spence unfolds, was an active spy during the First World War, who proclaimed the determination of the Irish nationalists, and published anti-Allied articles in the United States, in order to undermine, by outright absurdity and political hyperbole, the German Empire's efforts to obtain their slender pittance of foreign support.[2]

Consequently, whichever period we focus our attention upon, the operation of intelligence was exercised under the precise circumstances of the case; the general cultivation of military success, defense of diplomatic relations, and the acquisition of wealth, and, lastly, to maintain the order and peace of society. In other words, the consumers of intelligence found in it an obvious expedient for serving their interests true to the level of the situation: temporary and local, or permanent and altogether foreign. Meanwhile, it should be noted that after the world wars, as we can infer from the official history of the British intelligence community, intelligence is the only basis of obligation for the thousands of officers hired and every new organization established (which is frequently discovered to be in possession of a sizeable sum of annual money), under which they are conceived to invent and maintain the complex machine of intelligence-gatherers and -analyzers, counter-espionage wardens in particular, and the covert action functionaries, whose employment is perpetual, and whose subsistence is, for that reason, the result of their employment. Previously to the era of intelligence institutions, intelligence was no more than an ad hoc exertion of ambassadors, military attachés, mercenaries, codebreakers and codemakers, political assassins and saboteurs, to hold other nations at bay, to penetrate their secrets, to form alliances and counter-alliances, and to traverse their machinations. Indeed there is something extremely telling in finding senior intelligence figures today having access to their political overlords, in direct opposition to every other head of the government's permanent bureaucracy or secretariat. In pursuing this inquiry, the object of this chapter is to present a general outline of the functions of intelligence.

SPIRIT OF INTELLIGENCE

The Art of War, composed of 13 (surviving) chapters in the Late Spring and Autumn Period (roughly 771 to 476 BC) by the Chinese military strategist, Sun Tzu, will still be found to occupy perhaps the first place in the catalog of intelligence sources. Let us briefly recollect his understanding of the subject here. Sun Tzu thinks that if espionage is done to its merits, it includes the germ of ultimate victory. From this view of the subject military leaders shall better know the plans and intentions of their enemy: for in the absence of the intelligence concerned, they cannot perhaps be other than half-blind; whereas an equal absence of intelligence about their own affairs renders them wholly blind. After all, it ought not to be forgotten that, though violence and bloodshed have too often been coeval with victories of the military, the connection is not essential or requisite. Therefore, the duty of the true strategist is to prevail upon their enemies with minimal bloodshed. If they are constantly aware of this, their minds will glow with the philosophical accuracy of the Tao;[3] and, of course, it is a simple statement of fact when we observe that the operation of the general's mind seems to be comprised of, for the most part, all that a reflecting and impartial intelligence is accustomed to yield to the guidance of their knowledge.

THE INTELLIGENCE CYCLE

In the meantime, it is obvious to remark that the term intelligence, at the present time, would be understood to convey the most comprehensive sense that can be annexed to the word, including every conceptual tool that can give birth to a train of antecedents and consequents of which the intelligence community is capable. In this view, the theoretical regulation to which the outcome of intelligence ought to be conformed is usually called the Intelligence Cycle. The Intelligence Cycle, as has been frequently observed by specialists, consists entirely of five or six successive gradations, in the following manner: planning and direction; collection; procession and exploitation; analysis and production; dissemination and integration. The first of these is the determination of the intelligence requirement by the executive power in cultivating their civil and military object, upon which their instructions are founded. The second is the obtainment of information or data by direct or indirect sources and methods of operation: from human (HUMINT), signals (SIGINT), imagery (IMINT), geospatial (GEOINT), measurement and signatures (MASINT), and open-sources (OSINT). The third of the steps enumerated is that information is processed and collated to ascertain the relevance and reliability of the data they have already adopted. In the fourth place, the analysis of the whole collection of records, for the purpose of interpreting the weight of the subject, is evident. The fifth and last procedure necessary to be adverted to is that which delivers the final result of this cycle with a degree of assurance to their superiors through any proper channels, depending upon the urgency, and there were no defects to correct. As to the cycle itself, it must be admitted that the same process may be repeated indefinitely, because the consumer may see a reason to alter or improve their requirement.

COUNTERINTELLIGENCE

There is another sense in which intelligence must be admitted to be valid, and that is counterintelligence: it is an engagement to the cause of national defense to defy all the attempts which can be made to have access to the secrets of their state. So true is the observation of Peter Wright and Paul Greengrass, that 'It is no good planning decades ahead [...] because by the time you get two or three years down the track, you might find your project leaked.'[4] To illustrate this with an obvious example, the disclosure of the Berlin Tunnel in the early part of the Cold War (designed to allow the United State's Central Intelligence Agency and the United Kingdom's Secret Intelligence Service to listen to the communications of the Soviet Union in East Germany without notice) is an intelligence failure of considerable magnitude, if we reflect upon the loss of millions of dollars attendant upon this long-term project. And here we will recollect the Russians thus insinuated themselves into the administration of the work by the hand of George Blake, the Secretary of the Planning Committee within the walls of the Secret Intelligence Service.[5] In other cases, the path of counterintelligence seems visible and distinct in the sense of the provision for their defense against assassination, violent sabotage, or cyber attack by foreign or domestic powers, societies, and individuals. Hence, in securing their defenses, counterintelligence recurs less to the *passive* measures of 'security of classified material, personnel security, physical security, security education, communications security, data security, electromagnetic emission security, censorship, camouflage, concealment, light, and security discipline,' than to the *active* measures of 'counterespionage, countersabotage, countersubversion, counterterrorism, counterreconnaissance, concealment, and deception operations and vary with the mission and capabilities of the unit.'[6] A counterintelligence system must be regularly formed and evaluated; they must concert together; and the measures they execute may originate in the connection of one percipient source of intelligence with another, such as their double agents or informants, as well as many other intelligences in which they discover their security defects.[7]

COVER ACTION

COVERT ACTION

It is far from certain that, in the controversy brought forward by covert action 'to influence political, economic, or military conditions abroad,' or by plausible deniability to withhold any identity annexed to its operation, democracies altogether 'believe that secret means are the best way to achieve a desired end or a specific policy goal.'[8] Yet decades after the agitation of these controversies in the United States and the United Kingdom, covert action is still pregnant with the most mischievous activities, including propaganda, that is, the covert dissemination of 'specific information in order to achieve foreign policy goals;' particular actions that 'covertly influence the political or economic workings of a foreign nation;' paramilitary operations that 'covertly train and equip personnel to attack an adversary or to conduct intelligence operations;' and lethal action, such as political assassinations and cyber attacks, proportioned to the whole extent of the threat during times of war or conflict.[9] The secret war of the Special Operations Executive (SOE) in the Second World War supplies the most eligible example that may be adduced in the case of the United Kingdom.[10]

STRATEGIC DECEPTION

From a different perspective, we can review the history of intelligence and consider it an instrument to be applied in the deception of their enemy's mind. In that case, no introduction seems more proper to this inquiry than the willingness to intoxicate and mislead the depositories of political and military power, by false intelligence, through the means of delusive impressions, received from 'public or private statements by government officials, leaks to journalists, double agents, and spoofing of technical intelligence collection sensors.'[11] The success of an attempt to mislead depends upon the appreciation of 'the cognitive processes of the target decision makers or intelligence analysts,' and the counterdeception operations by which they detect the limitations that exist as to the utility of their information processing capabilities. Of the recommendations possessed by the latter, we find it amidst the well-known example perpetually exhibited, the Double-Cross System or xx System, planned and executed by the British Security Service (MI5) during the period of the Second World War, when captured spies from Nazi Germany were submitted in the sequel to connive at the propagation of the false and pernicious estimate of the intrinsic circumstances of the conduct of the United Kingdom upon their controller's table in the *Abwehr* or *Sicherheitsdienst des Reichsführers-SS*, and acting upon the dictates of their keepers. Much has been stated about Operation Fortitude's success in concealing the exact location of the Normandy landings, and it is amusing to note how completely Nazi Germany was duped by double spies.

The consequence, therefore, of admitting the full extent of the faculties of the intelligence community is attributing to intelligence an expectation to engage in a 'constant war,' and that it is fitted for the internal and external affairs of a nation.[12] Yet it is to be remembered that this view of intelligence did not, as now, derive its existence from the open bureaucracies who are appointed to its functions in almost every modern country, nor had its crude conceptions amended by the experience of successive discussions before the interdisciplinary academic field of intelligence studies began to unfold and establish certain general principles upon the subject. Thus the sense in which we have used the word *intelligence*, as descriptive of every variety of function taking place in any part of the intelligence community, will usefully occupy the remainder of the present volume.

ENQUIRY CONCERNING INTELLIGENCE

The second oldest profession, perhaps, is that of the spies.[13] But, in reality, what a strain of astonishment and terror, a concerted hypocrisy and conspiracy, an ambition of intrigue and secret influence, and a series of servility and cabal, does this scene present to the present state of modern times! Is this really an habitual state of the political ocean, or is it an institutional crisis in our history likely to remain unique? Can we believe that the individual shall enter upon this profession with so notorious a tolerance of disingenuity, and that no consequences will flow from the suppression of the understanding of the subject by the public at large in whose interests they receive a pecuniary recompense? There is no doubt that intelligence is no longer the 'missing dimension of most diplomatic history.'[14] In addition, we also seem to have a glimpse of how the 'civilizing of intelligence' opens a door to the revisal of our intelligence community. The direct and unambiguous road to the public esteem will be the cultivation of some species of ingenuity, or the display of the diversified modes of their conduct, and that the societies, where the whole of this question of intelligence has necessarily occupied a share in the disquisitions of all writers, will be treated as the most democratic state.

Having thus far investigated the nature of intelligence functions, I shall attempt to scrutinize, in detail in the following chapters, that mass of practical inferences that flow from it in moral and political calculation, and the method I adopt is to clear the ground, more rigorously than ever, penetrated by the genial dew of the soil in which socio-political-cul-tural melioration is found to germinate. In each successive chapter, our hypotheses, our avocations, and our proceedings will contribute to this end. So that the second chapter will anticipate the hypothesis of ethical intelligence; the third shall receive a more particular discussion of the sociological evidence of the positive effect of civilization into the field of intelligence; and, fourthly, we will observe that the legal weaknesses of cyberspace are not invincible. Then we have to enter, in the chapters of the second part of this book, more into the subject of intelligence oversight, especially that part of it which relates to intelligence effectiveness in democratic society, and the manner in which it is administered by the Intelligence and Security Committee in the Parliament of the United Kingdom. Lastly, in the appendix, we remind the reader of the significant changes which Liberalism has undergone as an intellectual being, and it is necessary they should be acquainted with the context that may therefore be interwoven with the establishment of institutional intelligence. Now let us attend to the result of the succeeding discussions.

CHAPTER II

OF THE DIFFERENCE OF MORALS:
CAN INTELLIGENCE EVER BE ETHICALLY SOUND?

According to prior reports, policymakers were put under enormous pressure to carry out their duties on national security following the brutal manner in which masses were killed in the unexpected horror that ensued on September 11, 2001. However, it may be alleged that some egregious persons, though not so many others, gave somewhat less than ordinary attention in this dimension to the morality of natural reason and its contrary vices.[15] With torture, the true moral philosophy of secret intelligence has now gained a reputation amongst the multitude to be debated and judged on a controversy between the courage to violate laws and oppressing the power to put them in execution. Therefore, notwithstanding the laws of their countries (Bill of Rights 1689, and UN Declaration on the Protection of All Persons from Being Subjected to Torture and Other Cruel, Inhuman or Degrading Treatment or Punishment 1975), intelligence agencies, from time to time, especially took advantage of torture, easily seduced by the pretense of the ticking bomb scenario

before them, because the peace and safety of the people require a 'taking of the sword' and torture could
be administered to all degrees of people.[16] As for the
difficulties of the contexture held significative of the
ticking bomb scenario, I intend to review and expose
them in this chapter. This will render it intelligible
to any modern tongue and reveal the whole scope of
the act of spying (apart from all other actions of intelligence: as covert action, surveillance, and counter-intelligence) as an ethically intended service in-
stituted by the consent of their country. The 'ticking
bomb scenario,' a hypothetical thought experiment,
appears to be a theorem addressing the most conducive motion to common peace and safety. In this
scenario, a terrorist is held captive, or in the power of
their allies, and by the terror of torture, is compelled
to betray a specific location, where they are to seek
and defuse a bomb to save civilians from death and
injury. We can deduce from this that it means that,
through some apparent procedure and instruction,
it promises to provide facts needed to quote any lo-
cations to find the bomb inside the time before the
detonation (as popularized in multiple episodes of
24, an action television series). For my part, when I
consider the moral laws in the West, I believe there
are two kinds of 'ideal-type' moral philosophies; one
is Deontological, and the other is Utilitarian. I will
boldly conclude that the arguments by which each
doctrine would prove that intelligence officials receive their jurisdiction from are all in vain, as there
appear, in this case, to be two contradictory laws.
Yet, in some cases, from contradictory voices, there
follows a third philosophical truth by logic in consequences of words, which is the Just Intelligence

Theory (JIT). When I have demonstrated the suffi-
ciency of JIT, I will conclude that intelligence and
ethics are consistent; the dictates of which are tolera-
ble in society as long as they weigh the objectives and
means with precise reasons.

RIGHT TO TORTURE WHENCE DERIVED

Before I infer anything from the right to torture,
I must first explain what is to be understood by
Utilitarianism. As Jeremy Bentham would pose (who
was one of the old Utilitarians), an action is laudable
if it has 'the greatest amount of good for the greatest number;' by *Summum Bonum* (greatest good) is
meant the greatest happiness;[17] which distinction he
observed in this doctrine, 'Nature has placed man-
kind under the governance of two sovereign masters,
pain and *pleasure*. It is for them alone to point out
what we ought to do, as well as to determine what
we shall do.'[18] Therefore, the damage done to happiness (or pleasure) by a free execution of malice will
always be regarded as a profoundly bad deed. And
though many places affirm the labor to procure
overall happiness, I find none affirming happiness in
individuals. As a result, it is possible that a subject
be sacrificed, for example, by being put to death in
order to please and thrill the assembled people, in
which case the judgment by the same authority is
said to be good and just.[19] As a result, the outcome
determined in this case is expressly confirmed as a
generally ethical act, despite the fact that a criminal
is sentenced to lose their dignity through torture.

Nevertheless, we are not to understand that Utilitarianism consists in uniformity: for those actions that are done for the present public interest proceed from a shorter-sighted craft called Act Utilitarianism; whereas that which Bufacchi and Arrigo call Rule Utilitarianism is a putting off of a present danger by engaging into a greater perspective. Rule Utilitarians prescribe and command the observation of those general rules and principles, that are otherwise called the Consequentialist Fallacy. As a result of their examination of the consequences that appear to them to be deducible from the act of torturing, the preparations for which are required from time to time for the well-being of multitudes, there must certainly be great caution against any irreversible normalization of torture as a state instrument; from which proceeds an emulation of a slippery slope towards that which tends to weaken the democratic doctrines maintained by so many institutions, which include their army, doctors and judges. The Rule Utilitarians' understanding is that when torture is commonly employed, the civil state may, in other situations, resort to the torture of innocent citizens and suffer many times the prosperity of the entire nation. The adversities of institutionalized torture as proceeding from a watchful observation of the diverse countries of Latin America, as in Chile (or of Africa, as in Algeria), demonstrate the truth that they have engaged themselves beyond hope of repair.

But yet, I think, the endeavor to advance a consistent doctrine of right and wrong should not be easily declared indisputable. For seeing the will of the Rule Utilitarian is a kind of doctrine, there appears on another occasion a contradictory voice from the greater number. The future of the nation is gotten by cautious rules; but what if the bomb could annihilate the whole nation *eo instante*? For if we could suppose this precept was not imaginary, I see no reason why to call it a 'rule' rather than an 'act,' seeing they need to break the force of their words for the assuring of continued life: which is as much as to say, that Utilitarianism, as to the whole doctrine, I do not see the principles of it are proper and the ratiocination solid. Torture, in the nature of Utilitarianism, proceeding only from a dissimilitude of inclinations and wills, becomes moral or immoral according to the design and obligations of every particular occasion therein. And thus, much is enough to have been said of the Utilitarians.

GOOD AND EVIL APPARENT

Knowing now what is the doctrine necessary to torture, we are to consider next concerning Deontology; what and why are the articles or points it commands necessary? So it appears plainly, to my understanding, that Deontology, whether the interest of one individual or assembly of individuals is concerned, proceeds from a peremptory pursuit of universal rules that accepts all the consequences. The Deontology-school will say it is grounded upon certain texts of Kant. In sum, all that is necessary to Kant is contained in his two Categorical Imperatives.

One, an act that is not universalizable is not moral, 'Act only according to that maxim by which you can at the same time will that it should become a universal law;'[20] that is to say, a person who refuses to take upon themselves a painful act cannot be said to wish it as a universal rule. And seeing every individual is presumed by reason to promote his own benefit, no one will be glad to be at ease with the menaces of torture. The other principle in Deontology is that members of every domain must treat one another as ends in themselves, not as the means and instruments towards an end, because every person is the author of whatsoever that so bear their person and are in all rights equal. So, when we imagine the ticking bomb scenario, a student of Deontology will abandon the protection due to their public, because it endeavors as much as it can, by force, to receive secret intelligence without the consent of the individual that is injured, who have the same rights as others, as 'means' towards the acquisition of intelligence; and because the attempt to gaining it so is destructive to their life as an end itself.[21]

From this equality of rights arises equality of hope in attaining the proper object of everyone's will. And therefore, if common people in their misfortunes lay the fault on inaction, neglect of the ticking bomb scenario would be a contradiction and impediment to the universalizable rule of Kant's law. From that second principle of the Categorical Imperative, by which we are obliged to yield obedience to the sovereignty of another in procuring the safety of their own body, holding this right as it were by entail inalienable, we are still in the condition of conflict of every right against every right. Here it is confirmed that the rights belong both to the terrorist and to all the people that shall die.[22] And hence it comes to pass that Deontology is a hard matter and thought impossible to distinguish exactly between good and evil, which is a confession that its irregular system is nothing but mere madness and the delusions of the infallibility of reason. It is evident that Kant's Deontology is not too free from the accidents of the brain to govern a whole body of ethical guidelines concerning intelligence affairs.

In sum, the discourse of the 'ideal-type' schools of philosophy, namely Utilitarianism and Deontology, when it is regulated by metaphorical designs, can expect nothing but to continually endeavor to secure themselves against contradictions and absurdities within themselves and between themselves. And particularly, in the question of the ticking bomb scenario, where there are no variable factors, neither Deontology nor Utilitarianism are equally applicable to any difficult question. Nevertheless, we are not to renounce the ends or resolutions of this discourse because there is indeed a school of philosophy by which they might succeed truly to resolve such things which make ill impressions in the minds of the people; and that is, the Just Intelligence Theory: which was derived from the clauses of the Just War Theory (JWT), of which I shall speak more particularly hereafter.

THE THIRD NORMATIVE FRAMEWORK,
JUST INTELLIGENCE THEORY

The properties of a just act in intelligence consist principally of two things; one is *jus ad intelligentiam*, or just resort to intelligence: the other is *jus in intelligentia*, or just execution of intelligence.[23] Allhoff applies the Just Intelligence Theory to the practice of torture and conceives it acceptable, within the bounds of the most strict material circumstances; which consist of absolute knowledge of the fact that the person held prisoner knows where the bomb is placed; that there are no other means of avoiding the torture, that it will attain their ends; and that torture proceeds from intention to prevent discord, not (for example) from any delight they can expect in the coercion or punishment of their subject.[24] The Just Intelligence Theory requires further that the ways and degrees of torture be minimally administered and exclude innocent subjects in the process of torture. When the Just Intelligence Theory is obeyed accordingly, then the act can properly be styled clean or just, or else they have the need to find other means.

But what then shall we say of the similitude of the aim of Utilitarianism to promote goodness, to the necessity of the Just Intelligence Theory to do the same? To answer hereunto, we are to seek the distinction in the utilitarian intention of the former doctrine. For the intention of Utilitarianism to maximize the overall utility, whether it will come to pass or not, is contrary to the first and fundamental law of JIT, which commands to seek just causes, which can by reason be either demonstrated or confuted.

Furthermore, seeing Rule Utilitarians weigh actions according to the security of the future happiness, though it is consequent to the condition, that there be no immediate peril to the safety of a whole nation, caused (for example) by a nuclear bomb. It follows manifestly that in all kinds of foretelling events, JIT has the flexibility of compromise, which criteria are set down in the knowledge of what is just and unjust, both in peace and war. In the same manner, the followers of Deontology, when they pretend to be the sole legislators of moral laws (such of them as they ordain to be universally agreed on), think they never do an injustice; and yet they do not question what other side there is of their obligation to innocents put to death by an other: there being nothing absolutely and simply in the like cases for ever after. On the other side, I have not found any doctrine that can deal proportionally according to precepts and limits prescribed by all extraordinary events, except the doctrine of JIT, the dictates whereof depend on much experience, discretion, evidence, and foresight of things to come.

Let us now consider what defects are contrary to the unity of JIT. In the same manner, as JWT has a need for an amalgamation of conceptions to prevent an arbitrary relapse in the condition of war: so also, notwithstanding the contrariety of some of its general rules, as also the connexions of its consequences to another, in civil troubles and calamities of the nation, JIT has need of principles grounded upon a presumption of difference and mutability.[25] By this, it is apparent that neither JWT nor JIT can feign to be infused or inspired by one foundational law that might cohere together articles of distinct signification, as legitimacy, proportionality, discrimination, and justifiability: in which case, every subject that is obliged to converse in hard questions of an abstruse philosophy, that is, to discern exactly between right and wrong, may nevertheless in many occasions have nothing at all to answer, but are destitute of those lenses that see well enough the way of righteousness in the approach of danger. Michael Quinlan also regards the general impediment of drawing the line, where human nature is in continual motion and can never be made quantifiable as in mathematics.[26] And consequently, there is no longer a clear guide to those incidents that converse in questions of matters corporeal. To this might be added this, that as the ticking bomb scenario has no existence, but in the fiction of the mind: so the unlikely images of critics, rising from the representations of their own fancies, consist only in fixed variables and premises, such as are all things incorporeal. I will add only to this interpretation that the logician adds together many syllogisms to make a settled demonstration: that the practice of all intelligence agencies cannot be unjust, that the measure of good and evil actions, and the establishment of their policy must therefore be determined by the worldly business of the nation, rather than that of the abstractions of our minds. Seeing then that what is best to be done consists in thought experiments that simply renounce the obscure, confused, and ambiguous expressions of the world, the ticking bomb scenario is (as often as people are sensible of its effects) censured for a false presumption of its grounds, or principles of reason: that whatsoever is the object, there is small probability any torture has had success in history (the only corroboration of matter of fact).[27] Again, if we speak in the abstract, we shall suppose torture is conducive to such a benefit, that it has in its power to save or destroy lives.

PURGATORY FOR THE SPOOK, HOWSOEVER UNDERSTOOD

The difference between the differing kinds of intelligence activities consists not in the difference of decorum, but in the difference of essence, which is not without contention: in so much as covert action, as sabotage, assassinations, support for subversion, support for *coups d'état*, and the like (which violate by the way another nation's autonomy and independence, as well as give such authority to subject themselves to normative future domestic operations; as for example, Operation CHAOS) would need nothing but the agreement of JIT to proceed to execution. And therefore, it seems to be that permission would extend to all other acts of the intelligence community. Be that as it may, I cannot forbear to observe the interesting fact that even if all the aforementioned arguments were rejected outright, it is still possible to produce an argument to defend intelligence, to a great extent, as in the exercise of passive faculties, consisting of analytics, cyber security, vetting, or collection of open-source intelligence, and others; whereby no person will approach the pain of violence and robbery. So that to them that can see the connexion of those means, the metaphorical signification of intelligence may be called the 'shield' of the nation, whereas the contrary may generally be the offensive 'sword.'[28] In that sense, I see no argument that proves intelligence, as a flexible term naturally consequent to the essence of the activity in question, is agreeable to the harmony and scope of any school of ethics. To conclude, the light of intelligence activities, sufficiently informed, is mental discourse purged from ambiguity. From thence, the Just Intelligence Theory is the way; case-by-case assessment, the pace; and the increase of justice, the end; whereas on the contrary, Deontology and Utilitarianism are like *ignes fatui*, and resting upon them is reckoning among contentious absurdities: and their end, mutiny against their governors. For seeing nature is contrary to that strict distinction which some make between black and white, it is manifest that JIT is a method of seeking the purifying fire of Purgatory in a world of large grey areas, where Deontology and Utilitarianism ought, therefore, to supplement it, by providing the guidance of pure reason, not to mention knowledge of the consequences of events appertaining to the intelligence activity in hand. According to this sense, we are to remember that this chapter proceeded from an intention to examine and try out the imposture of the train of syllogisms concerning fictitious operations. As for the instance of securing the conditions of JIT, it is not sufficiently evident that it will be easy, or perhaps possible; there being nothing in human life that makes it simple, for they are singular and individual. By this imposition of material circumstances, whatever quality makes an intelligence activity ethically sound is not so easy to assent to, and sometimes more particularly, the part of it caused by the succession of new technologies and forms of intelligence. Let us now consider the 'civilizing of intelligence' and what it is that preserves and dissolves it.

CHAPTER III

AN INTERDISCIPLINARY INVESTIGATION: THE CIVILIZING PROCESS AND THE STUDY OF INTELLIGENCE

The 'missing dimension' of international relations is perhaps the most common phrase associated with the study of intelligence.[29] Essentially, it refers to the neglect of the effect of intelligence activities on the conduct and outcome of inter-state intercourse. In fact, it is not unusual that some, particularly those who may flirt with conspiratorial fancies, claim that the secret world of espionage is the chief force behind all the multifarious events of our political history. Undoubtedly, these are bloated exaggerated claims that cannot withstand the critical rules of logic. In any case, the purpose of this chapter is not to discuss these matters. What it will do, rather, is to approach the 'study of intelligence' in an interdisciplinary manner: that is, from the point of view of what sociologists call Eliasian studies, a field of knowledge introduced by Norbert Elias, the ingenious author of *The Civilizing Process*, as well as one of the earliest advocates of process sociology, a certain methodological frame and system that, in short, terminates the perceivable distance between any one individual and their society. To satisfy this inquiry, I will appeal to the two theories of International Relations, which are most frequently considered, classical realism and the English School, as our starting point. Divided into four sections, this chapter shall sequentially review Elias' 'elimination contests' (and 'state formation') and the role of intelligence within these processes; the 'society of states' as propounded by the English School and the existence of what may be called the 'society of intelligence agencies;' Elias' civilizing process and its implications on the similar pattern of the 'civilizing of intelligence;' and finally, the overall position of intelligence studies within the Eliasian literature. It is important to point out the topic at hand and our findings are unprecedented. There are no scholarly texts that explore the connexion between intelligence activities and Eliasian themes.[30] It is hoped, therefore, that by the end of this project, the outcome should not only enrich the academic study of intelligence but should also make further progress towards knowledge of Elias' 'civilizing process.'

In any case, before I proceed to what I think on this subject, it is first important to clarify what is meant by intelligence. This is crucial because intelligence, in its entirety, is a large and immense field that we cannot easily define in a sentence. It suffices to my present discourse to state here that intelligence signifies 'processed' (or analyzed) information used by policymakers for policymaking purposes, not to mention their national security a little more particularly.[31] Indeed, intelligence is unique in the sense that it is secretly received from human or technological sources.[32] Of especial emphasis, to which historians generally refer, there are offensive and defensive purposes that serve intelligence agencies: offensively, it is usually used to defeat an enemy by finding out their weaknesses (in military operations, for exam_-ple), whereas defense (called counter-intelligence) consists in neutralizing whatever efforts enemy espionage would make in order to gain insight into their secret data (that is, to prevent the exposition of their weakness that will follow naturally from the promiscuous use of secret knowledge left half open); but also, by that means, to preempt their causing disorder in, or bringing mischief upon, their national security. Needless to say, intelligence can addition-ally refer to covert action, i.e., a number of different activities (including, *inter alia*, murder, propaganda, and monetary support to militias), each of which is an invasion or violation of the sovereignty of another state or non-state actor. With these truths in mind, as each of the aforementioned ways of intelligence concern the topic of this treatise, it makes common sense to define intelligence by the different contexts it converses with.

INTELLIGENCE AND PROCESS SOCIOLOGY, CONSIDERED TOGETHER

Having thus laid down these premises concerning intelligence in general, let us return to our subject matter. This section surveys the role of intelligence in state formation and elimination contests. Elias, who inquired after the development of accepted code of manners and social behaviors of our Western European states since the Middle Ages, tells us that elimination contests and state formation result from the increasing tendency of 'centrifugal' forces to gradually give way to 'centripetal' forces, by which train of events power is centralized in the hands of the sovereign, but none in those of nobles, knights, or other local centers of power that environ the central authority.[33] Additionally, with this hypothesis, two processes occur in concurrence with their tempo and inclination: viz. the centralization of taxation and instruments of violence.[34] Then the consequence is that state borders gradually came to be defined more clearly around the king (hence, state formation), having also increased the struggle between neighboring kings at the same time (hence, elimination contests). Kings now needed to fight other kings to ensure their own survival and to prevent the expansion of the other kings. To extend his thoughts a little further, Elias observes that all such patterns put them – but not always – in the direction of their particular overarching centripetal force, which is the means to obtain a general monopoly, and to be that which people would everywhere are encompassed with, whose peaceful co-existence no one can deny; there being no question of elimination contests. Admittedly, in what concerns us, there is little or no difference between Eliasian sociology and classical realism.[35] Both seem to agree on the idea that self-interest, and the conveniences of some violent impression on other states, are because of the 'anarchic' nature of the world, besides the operation of survival mechanisms that do really exist in the states themselves, which fear is, as a matter of fact, founded upon what realists call the 'security dilemma.' So also finding that the highly emotion-driven 'double-bird process,' which is a certain development of state responses in relation to their perception of other countries, forces them to rely on the progressive build-up of instruments of physical force. Indeed, Elias says much about this matter, especially when it concerns the centralization of taxation and instruments of war. Surprisingly, however, despite the role played by espionage in international relations (particularly in the way familiar to realists) and in these patterns, there is no mention of intelligence activities in the field of process sociology. Therefore, the next paragraph shall handle propositions that attempt to fill this gap by way of illustrating the ways whereby intelligence affects state formation and elimination contests.

According to Jock Haswell, intelligence in the Middle Ages was chiefly used for military purposes. For example, heralds (who were experts in 'lineage and coats of arms') were used by local commanders to 'read' enemy shields and inform them about knights who opposed them.[36] Of course, the most important purpose in this instance was the identification of their enemy because knights were 'completely encased in steel,' meaning only their supporters knew who they were (each knight having his unique 'arms' laid upon his shield). What this suggests is that the role of intelligence in the monopolization of power and state formation was, at the time, in the recognition of these knights who opposed centripetal forces; intelligence was the great instrument of 'policing' in the struggle against domestic centrifugal forces around the king. This primary quality is observed by Peter Gill and Mark Phythian in England, wherein 'the development of systems of intelligence was rooted in the protection of the crown and the uncovering of plots against it.'[37] That being said, the role of intelligence extended to foreign affairs (and thus external elimination contests) as well. For instance, the intelligence collected by Sir Francis Walsingham (Queen Elizabeth I's spymaster and principal secretary) was crucial in saving the monarchy and its realms from the Armada, which King Philip II of Spain planned to send to the English Channel. It is interesting to note, however, that the Spanish, too, had their own intelligence networks, which they used for both offensive and defensive purposes (though, clearly, they failed to succeed in either).[38] What is noteworthy is that this pattern has existed and evolved for a continued duration in the West, and therefore it is possible may extend to periods to come. In fact, intelligence has evolved to such a degree that Allen Dulles, the first civilian director of central intelligence (DCI), viewed intelligence as the main instrument of opposition against 'Communism.' Certainly, even though his beliefs were shaped in reference to the Cold War, these patterns have not since changed much, and one will perceive demonstrative evidence in the world that national intelligence systems are considered the first line of defense against external and internal threats. What needs to be drawn from this argument, then, is that despite certain irregularities in the use of intelligence since the Medieval Ages, intelligence appears

to have contributed continuously to elimination contests and state formation – though to varying degrees
in each instance – which seems to me at least to in-
timate the confession that intelligence is inseparable
from the 'civilizing process.'

IDEALIST PROPOSITIONS:
THEIR MIXED MODES AND RELATIONS

The neglect of the role of intelligence in elimination
contests and state formation is not the only quality
absent from Elias' 'civilizing process.' As Andrew
Linklater points out, Elias' 'realist' approach to international relations does not reflect the idea of a
'society of states,' as the English School suspects.[39] In
short, a 'society of states' refers to a continual cooperation between two or more actors who have come
nearer each other by, for instance, their shared values, goals, ideals, cultural and linguistic characteristics.[40] Historical instances that may serve to illustrate
this observation consist of those notions concerning
Hellas in Ancient Greece, the 'court society' (or 'civilized' diplomatic relations) of Europe (specifically
those in Western Europe) before and during the Age
of Enlightenment, and today the European Union
– as is shown in other places. What is less obvious,
however, is that such kind of close relations may
also expand into other domains. I am referring on
this occasion to a concept of a broader extension;
the new term 'society of intelligence agencies.' The
Five Eyes furnishes us with an example worth taking notice of,[41] as an intelligence alliance comprising

the spy agencies of Britain, Canada, Australia, New Zealand, and the United States. This 'society' is unique as it reflects Martin Wight's definition of a 'society of states' above mentioned: viz. that their respective intelligence agencies within their own state share similar goals, values, cultural and linguistic features, and have continuously cooperated with one another on intelligence matters since the beginning of the Cold War. Naturally, such a general definition may suggest that the creation of the Five Eyes was, in the first place, because of their shared characteristics. Undoubtedly, this perspective makes a part of our complex story. However, upon due examination, Elias' understanding of the 'court society' shows us a more improved comprehension of intelligence alliances.

Earlier, it was pointed out that 'state formation' developed with a lessening of 'centrifugal forces' and a greater increase of 'centripetal forces' within their territory. It was also noted that this process happened in a line parallel to 'elimination contests' between neighboring kings, who feared for their own security and survival. But what did not receive sufficient explication was how these processes drew people together within a territory. Hence, to defeat an external enemy and to prevent their extinction, members of a state needed to entertain and submit to internal pacification, as many did out of the ordinary road.[42] As Elias articulated, their reliance on one another (such as they found interconnectedness) meant that the occupants of a realm had to 'attune' to the needs and interests of their neighbors. Broadly speaking, he saw the connexion of this intermediate idea with 'court society:' the notion that former warriors and knights became less violent and developed superior ranks of behavior (in their attitudes and manners) within their king's court.

So said, it may be observed that the Five Eyes alliance displays similar patterns. For, under the circumstances of the Cold War, one of the greatest elimination contests in history, it was inevitable that participant states feared for their survival, so far as they felt the want of interdependence upon those who shared key qualities and faced the same enemy at the same time, proceeding from situations that, when reflected on, progressively (and continuously) led to a way of attuning their will to the needs and interests of their 'allies.' The same members of the Five Eyes are not so far from this discourse. It is true the perception of danger annexed to the Soviet Union (since its inception) was such that, though it processed slowly, each of the five members came together, and much more so by the momentum and other obliging circumstances that did not fail to accompany the Cold War to form an agreement in the allocation of secret information (in succession vitally united to their security), without being commissioned from an above political organization, like the EU – and might properly be termed a 'society of intelligence agencies.'

But, be that as it will, it is important to ask a very crucial question: why is it that despite facing the same professed enemy of their peace, the Five Eyes alliance has not extended to other Western democracies? To which I answer, we should return

to Elias, who gives a sociological account of 'established-outsider relations.' A little consideration of
a historical instance or two may make this inquiry
clear. According to Elias, the court society of France,
which developed on all sides of the one absolute
monarch (centralized monopoly of power), set the
standard of all other civilized (diplomatic) relations
betwixt distinct European courts.[43] The consequence of this development was very clear, viz. these
European courts started to recognize each other as
more civilized than the other countries, whose type
of 'diplomatic' relations with one another did not
agree to their particular palate. The conduct of their
diplomacy being thus distinguished and understood,
they termed one 'civilized' and the other 'barbarian.'
It is clear that a similar type of process seems to
be behind the creation of the Five Eyes. It is notable, for instance, that the five members express the
same *modus operandi*, whilst the United Kingdom's
agencies framed the standard during the two world
wars (especially in relation to their superb signals
intelligence) and long before that (in relation to their
'policing' of the colonies), and so manifestly demon-
strating the agreement (with 'established' group) or
disagreement (with 'outsider' group) of long-term
bonds and similitudes led to the creation of their
'society of intelligence agencies,' which necessarily
excluded the intelligence organizations of other
western democracies – consisting almost wholly in
distinct intelligence systems or even, say, cultures.[44]

But, as with relationships they had known
before, the bonds that hold members of a group

together may be broken; put differently, the feeling of interdependence is not always sufficient to 'eternalize' peace amongst their constituent members. One recent example illustrates this observation clearly. At the latter end of the 2000s, it was alleged that Britain's spy agencies (to be specific, the Secret Intelligence Service) was involved in the torture and extraordinary rendition of Binyam Mohamed, a British citizen who was tortured in Pakistan (despite clear judicial regulations forbidding the United Kingdom to consent to or to be complicit in acts of torture by its allies) and sent to Guantanamo Bay (again, with the agency's complicity).[45] Of what concernment the investigations of the judiciary may be, the court's demand to release classified documents regarding the case is convincing evidence: files abounded with all sorts of top secret information about its partners, and proceeding from their want of complete secrecy, the US government opposed this court order and made known to the government that they did not accept the public release of these documents: since otherwise they would find it almost unavoidable to 'reduce' intelligence sharing. Although this did not ultimately occur, it did demonstrate how interconnected dependencies between intelligence agencies could quickly come under attack if members started to feel the uneasiness of threats to their safety.

Admittedly, there is much to be said in this section. But as I mentioned earlier, these are only preliminary findings, and much research may be needed if we should add larger comprehension to this emerging field. With that earnest contemplation fixed and carried along in our minds, the next thing to be weighed is the other part of the apparent congruity of the works of intelligence and the civilizing process.

CIVILIZED INTELLIGENCE AND ITS DISTINCT IMPERFECTIONS

Having examined the history of intelligence, it is · to me intelligible that there are patterns containing the increase of oversight over intelligence agencies in democratic countries. Stated so, though there are numerous volumes of commentaries on the subject of intelligence oversight, yet none appear to have made the connexion with the 'civilizing process.' What is meant by the 'civilizing process' has already been touched on to some degree (especially when we discerned how interconnectedness might attain their peaceful interaction one to another). On the other side, Elias relates that after long intervals of time, the various peoples of Western Europe express less and less violent (or 'uncivilized') attitudes and manners, whilst, after such definition, they abhor those who do so – the Holocaust is the most prominent instance of the shock of the association of uncivil actions. Whether there is a long series of regular civilizing motions in the West remains to be seen. There is nothing more evident than that, in the framing of this section's present purpose, there is a train of figurative events which we could suppose as an attribute of the 'civilizing process' if we were to admit that it extends itself to the field of espionage – though it is uncertain that it does advance forwards *ad infinitum*, as happens in the case of organic 'processes' both ways, backwards and forwards.

The case against torture, I think, serves best to instance this viewpoint. Torture is known to be a method of intelligence collection (however ineffective) that some countries would have their spy organizations use, and, needless to enumerate, as it appears in all history. It is also easy to notice how torture was acceptable to the mind of man, wherein sophisticated torture devices were left branded upon the records of history. What is notable is that such violent operations gradually became less prevalent. Hence, in the latter end of the 19th century, there were causes of positive ideas according to common opinion; viz. the introduction of international conventions to protect human rights, whereas of late many people have had the pertinence to voice opposition against particulars wherein torture has allegedly happened, e.g., Guantanamo Bay and Abu Ghraib. Hence it will follow that their refreshed legislative framework has contributed to hindering the ill application of torture.

Either way, the 'civilizing of intelligence' should not be taken for granted, however. In the same way that the 'civilizing process' undergoes 'decivilizing processes,' so the 'civilizing of intelligence' could encounter the reverse process. For to return again to torture, it may be noticed that its prohibition has been cumbered and that, sometimes, there is evidence of motion carried away from 'civilizing' tendencies. Whether we can determine the direct involvement of our intelligence agencies or not, the torture of detainees in Guantanamo Bay and Abu Ghraib is an undeniable cogent demonstration of the 'decivilizing processes' in intelligence. It is true 'decivilizing processes' need not necessarily be separate from 'civilizing processes.' Krieken's observation, drawn from particulars into the maltreatment of Australian Aboriginal peoples by the colonists, who never suffered the civilizing mission to be otherwise mentioned but as the foundation and basis on which they disseminated their civilized manners, customs, and fashions, must show that civilizing and decivilizing processes can run simultaneously alongside one with another. So, with respect to the act of torture, Linklater tells us that in the aftermath of the September 11 attacks, such combinations of ideas as the 'protection' of civilization from the perceived 'outsiders,' viz. Islamic extremists attempted to implicitly persuade Western populations to accept the possibility of doing violence to them.[46] The analyses Tanja Collet made with Bush's post-9/11 speeches ought to be looked at as an illuminating instance concerning this kind of justification.[47]

But, before I conclude this section, there remains yet another more general, though perhaps less observed, connection between the signification of 'psychogenesis' and the 'civilizing of intelligence.' It is about the surveillance of the operation of bodies and minds by our spy agencies – it being unavoidable in discourses wherein the secrets of indiscriminate surveillance by the National Security Agency (NSA) and Government Communications Headquarters (GCHQ) were laid open by Edward Snowdon.

Surveillance uses appropriated technological techniques and methods, e.g., video surveillance (CCTV), data mining, and long-term digital storage houses, which 'intrude' by degrees into the private affairs of citizens within their countries. For, let it be ever so true that the greatest part of Western peoples are opposed to these measures, though less than to make their opposition be perceived in public. What is noticeable, nonetheless, is that the reasons whereof may be reduced to Elias' conception of fear or, as he puts it, sensibilities towards 'shame and embarrassment', which is a proper object of changes in people's manners and attitudes since the Medieval Ages.[48] Elias, by observing the changes in their mind and modes of actions, distinguished by their daily behaviors and acquired habits (by fashion, example, and education), viz. spitting, nose-blowing, and table manners, perceived that people perhaps contrary to their volition gradually come to prefer the 'privatized' suppression of their impulses, instead of unrestrained behavior. R. V. Jones (a former military intelligence expert during World War II), in his admired reflections, we find some kind of affirmation concerning this matter, as we can witness in this passage:

> Apart from the nightmare of a "Big Brother" state there is an *instinctive* dislike of surveillance, even parental surveillance; and there may well be an *apprehension* based deeply back in the *evolutionary process* arising from a feeling of *vulnerability* while *executing bodily functions* or in sickness, and of latent trouble from a stalking predator whose staring eyes betray his intentions (italics for emphasis).[49]

Therefore, we find the familiar debate concerning Elias' insights into long-term changes in people's manners and their gradual dislike of vulnerability, i.e., the feelings of 'shame and embarrassment' whenever they perform bodily functions. It is very likely, if not always, that all the long-term alterations Elias observes in his understanding of the 'civilizing process' may have influenced, in a very great 'processual' sense, people's perception of surveillance by their intelligence agencies (and police organizations). This connexion, I grant, seems to be self-evident, even though it is still worth bearing in mind that it will need further inquiries, perhaps, for instance, people's 'precise' notion of surveillance, censorship, etc., in the previous centuries.

OF THE IMPROVEMENT OF ELIASIAN STUDIES, OR VICE VERSA

Before I close this chapter, it may help if we take a little more exact survey of the 'position' of intelligence relative to Eliasian studies – to see, in other words, the ways whereby the study of intelligence may benefit his idea of the 'civilizing process.' So far, it seems to me that the aforementioned propositions chiefly contributed to the study of intelligence – by perusing the studies of 'civilizing processes,' its methodologies, and process sociology in general. It can only be a fair examination, therefore, if we return to what was discussed at the beginning of the essay about the role of intelligence in 'elimination contests' and 'state formation.' In short, it was shown how intelligence contributed to the monopolization of state power, both in terms of foreign threats as well as internal threats. Upon this ground, one may conjecture that the addition of another process, called the 'centralization of information-gathering capabilities and policing functions,' must have a place amongst Elias' axioms, viz. the centralization of taxation and instruments of violence. Yet, I suspect this notion may breed confusion since intelligence is better described in terms of the centralization of the instruments of violence for domestic policing (security) or to destroy foreign threats (war), and thus the domain of the instruments of physical force. Needless to say, states consider intelligence as being actually the first line of defense. This suggests, on the whole, that the study of intelligence will, most likely, benefit the 'civilizing process' only in terms of adding depth and detail to the above processes – instead of 'revolutionizing' it.

To conclude, there is much to be added and learnt from an interdisciplinary approach betwixt the two seemingly unrelated fields of intelligence studies and Eliasian studies. Of course, as far as this project attempted an investigation for this purpose, I hope it may be a reason to lead future research on the subject. But despite showing the vast extent of the field, it may suffice to have scratched its surface here merely by making an acquaintance with four themes:

1. The role of intelligence in elimination contests and state formation.

2. The preliminary introduction and examination of what we call the 'society of intelligence agencies' (drawing from the premises in the English School as the obliging context and Elias'

understanding of the interconnectedness and 'established-outsider relations' as the substance).

3. Introducing into discourse the so-called 'civilizing of intelligence' by way of considering or comparing the 'civilizing process' and the use of torture, not to forget surveillance as case studies.

4. And finally, a brief comment on the benefits of the study of intelligence to the Eliasian discourses.

Certainly, this is not an exhaustive list and does not include other areas where the two fields may find the benefit of this way – indeed, one example would be to explain the distrust within intelligence agencies between analysts and spies by referring to Elias' established-outsider relations (and the stigmatizations involved). In any case, perhaps a more important implication of this essay is how it demonstrates the advantages other disciplines can gain by investigating Eliasian thought in its different aspects and how the list of such disciplines may not be so easily exhaustible. As a final word, Elias' *The Civilising Process* and other works are truly groundbreaking and need to be drawn from extensively if they are to reach their true potential.

CHAPTER IV

THE EFFECT WHICH AN HETEROGENOUS
ASSOCIATION OF TECHNOLOGICAL
DEVELOPMENTS AND PRACTICES,
SUCH AS CYBERCRIME, HAS UPON
NATIONAL AND INTERNATIONAL LAW

In the present state of things in 'cyberspace', it appears to be necessary to go back to first prin-ciples. Probably the prevailing opinion of the electronic medium has taken its rise from Gordon Moore's law; true to his position as the co-founder of Intel Corporation in 1968, Moore's law apostrophiz-es that 'the number of transistors per square inch on integrated circuits' doubles every two years; and, uttering the apotheosis of our state of attainments, he exalts the exponential acquirement of techno-logical growth, rising superior to any other history of peoples.[50] It has also been asserted, by some tech-nologists, that information technology, together with the systems which bind cyberspace, for exam-ple, the World Wide Web, is at the forefront of this vigorous development. But, the rapid development of cyberspace is very problematical; for a numerous list of writers insist that all its aspects be subjected to national or international law best adapted to their time, place, and occasion. Yet, I will venture to affirm that their impassioned despisers will not acquire sufficient influence to enable them to deregulate the cybersphere from all government interference whilst making legal changes in the world is the first wish of the majority of policymaking circles. I am naturally led by this disputation to the main subject of the present chapter, and I shall attempt to illustrate some of the legal implications of the cyber domain with respect to cybercrime, cyber espionage, and cyber war. I wish, therefore, to form principles on a broad basis instead of being narrowed by artless modesty. The understanding of the whole tenor of the dispensations of the medium allows us no alternative. In tracing the opinions that occur in various academic writings, I have confined my findings to such as act upon the circumstances of the West, especially the laws relative to the Anglosphere.

THE INVOLVED OPINIONS OF LAW FOR CYBERSPACE CONSIDERED

After surveying the history of information technology and viewing the dangers of the Internet of Things so strenuously inculcated on the people of the Global North, exclamations against a well-regulated cyber domain, are to be found amongst any class of thinkers who promote its free flow of information and noninterference from other stalking mischiefs.[51] Their lively imagination, to apply the historical page, draws the picture of public freedom and universal transparency, with the consequent regard for

the progress of accountability and knowledge, con-
demned in a world like this, to prove the noble origin of the internet (or the World Wide Web); ever
pursuing what they acknowledge to be an important
method of fixing sound principles of democracy in
the superstructure of society till they all melt into difficulties with which humanity is attended. Yet such
undoubtedly attractive notions are not founded on
the knowledge that the present state of society, in the
first consideration of things, pervades information
technology at large: so the herculean dangers and
difficulties peculiar to their society are already apparent in this medium. In other words, the artificial
structure which enables people to carry their content
in this world into another world, cannot long deny
them their flaws. Until the manners of the times are
changed and formed on more reasonable laws, it may
be impossible to obtain good conduct in the cyber
relations of the people that occupy these domains.[52]

When contending for the rights of citizens,
their main argument for the use of the law is built on
this principle: if they are prepared by law to prevent
people from committing gross crimes, then, without
being gifted with a prophetic spirit, they venture
to predict that the restrain of law, however weak,
will render the practice of cybercrime (trafficking
in child pornography and intellectual property,
committing fraud, stealing identities, or violating
privacy) more difficult.[53] Indeed, some of these individuals or groups might be prevented from pursuing
the crime in cybersphere, and others may not have
had the chance to escape in this way from persecu-
tion; is not that legal framework then very defective

and very unmindful of the security of its members? For instance, take the example of Dmitry Sklyarov, a former employee of ElcomSoft (a security firm headquartered in Moscow), who in 2001 sold de- cryption codes for the Abode Reader eBook Reader, was arrested by the FBI, but could not be sentenced guilty in the end.[54] This dry caution may, it is true, protect society against the pernicious effects which arise from every vice; but will preclude people en- tirely abandoned in a state nearer to the chaos and disorder which prevail on them to materially injure the free discharge of information in any sense of the words. The only solid foundation for an orderly whole appears to be the course of law, the harmony of which arises from a balance of the proportion between freedom and security; this claim, if it is an emanation of J. S. Mill's classic liberalism, is insepa- rable from their democratic propensities.

Nevertheless, if it were on account of the Latin saying, *quis custodiet ipsos custodes?* (or, who will guard the guards themselves?), it may be observed that to protect civilians from any Orwellian tyranny which their state spreads, they must be dependent on laws that render the social compact truly equi- table. Edward Snowden's revelations of the PRISM, for instance, showed the surveillance program was both grossly indelicate and dangerous, and has had an even more fatal effect on the right to privacy of the people of English-speaking nations.[55] Thus, they have at least an opportunity to exert a legal system of checks and balances to assert their rights or claim the privileges of moral beings. Such are the efforts of international institutions, as they are at present conducted, that they should seek information and set their understanding to work on proper legal frameworks that strengthen civil rights internationally against state-sponsored abuses.[56] The same law (e.g., Freedom of Information Act), undoubtedly, in several respects, enhances democratic intercourse better than, strictly speaking, the disputable method of whistleblowing like WikiLeaks' news leaks – which, in all its ways, promised to enhance transparency and accountability, if not so successfully.[57] Hence, we have a good reason to establish information technology law: in which we would advance, instead of retarding, the flow of 'horizontal' and 'vertical' information.

THE SAME TOPIC COMPREHENSIVELY CONSIDERED

Many laws, however, may be unprepared for cyberspace's difficulties, especially the laws relative to foreign countries and the consideration of its comprehensive interconnections. So notorious is this fact, that seldom, if ever, states will wish to extradite cyber criminals residing in their borders, regardless of all legal distinctions. Contrary to their real interest on an enlarged scale, Kristan Stoddart declares that even the closest allies cannot be expected to cooperate; remember that the proceedings concerning Gary McKinnon were an example of Britain's refusal to deport to the United States a British citizen, who was accused of hacking their military and the National

Aeronautics and Space Administration's (NASA) computers.[58] This difficulty, naturally increased by local judicial frameworks as well as clashing interests – I mean in a politico-strategic sense – draws attention to the absence of international institutions that combine to enforce international law; it will also require the majority, if not all, of nation-states to agree that they act according to the same law.

Still, there are some loopholes out of which a perpetrator may creep, notwithstanding very strong laws and enforcement agencies, because it would be an endless, speculative task to trace the variety of co-inciding 'digital fingerprints' into which investigators are plunged – as some researchers exclaim.[59] Besides, to reason on Yoram Dinstein's ground, how can they be expected to attribute the errors of a computer to its creator or the 'man in the loop?'[60] No doubt too, what a strong barrier the rapid development of technology is, making at the same time a fervid increasing cybersphere when it stands in the way of an up-to-date law – and the time will inevitably come – but it cannot easily be reconciled without cultivating time, money and precedent in a great degree. Hence, we must either allow these irrefragable arguments, or treat with contempt the innovator's hand; were it abolished, governments would be entirely separated from external oversight (as might quickly be demonstrated by the practice of their surveillance programs), and I question whether they would become better administrators by sacrificing people's capacity to protect their well-being and freedom against them.

The fact is, however, that the supporters of cybersecurity laws and regulations may expect from law, what law cannot give. A sagacious state may strengthen the body of law and sharpen the instruments by which it is obeyed, but the honey must be the reward of the cyber domain's own compatibility with the same law. It is almost absurd to attempt to make this law relative to the alien structures of cybersphere with pharisaical exactness, because they are built on partial experience.[61] Be that as it may, a law, as Marion Nancy ventures to assert, that preys secretly on the expanding information technology networks, and turns to order the chaos which should otherwise mount with vigor in the cyberspace border, could inspire symbolic affections and great mechanisms against the seeds of vice.[62] But, let me stress, while laws have been decked with mechanical relations that enable them to bind society, short-lived as it may be on account of the root causes of crime (social, political, cultural, or economic), it would seem that they can produce a normative effect on long-term behavior, insisted upon as an undoubted taboo, crying out against every violation of justice.

ANIMADVERSIONS ON THE DEGRADATION
OF NATIONAL CYBERSECURITY

I shall now contrast the law of cybercrime with the law of national cybersecurity. All in all, there are two modes of attack: cyber sabotage or subversion, and cyber espionage.[63] The former attempts attacks on critical national infrastructures (namely, power grids, water supplies, and financial systems) and is most feared by industrial countries where information technology is established (certainly, the US is sometimes considered as the most vulnerable nation-state in cyberspace). The latter mode of cyber attack aims at stealing information from military or civilian establishments; for example, the allegations that China undermined the intellectual property of corporations in the United States by stealing their information on research and development of products and goods illustrates this remark.[64] So if industries or private companies had any sense, they would not fail to pursue cybersecurity above, or on a par with, the common standard. Hence Richard A. Clarke and Robert K. Knape deduce the Defensive Trinity from the three essential components of national security in cyberspace, which consist of the internet's backbone (i.e., internet service providers), critical national infrastructure (e.g., power grid), and state defense (departments, agencies, and other public bodies).[65] As for the usefulness of law in this respect, which has been echoed by several writers, Andrew Nolan actually advised the federal government of the United States to contribute to cybersecurity in these particulars by writing laws that require internet service providers, corporations, industries, and other state bodies across the country to implement better security, operate attentively, participate in cyber information sharing schemes, not to mention the introduction of compulsory programs for staff that raise their awareness of cyber threats.[66]

But, though cybersecurity should only be the natural reflection of the nation's priority, yet, when various technological advances have produced new mediums of war, which are very nearly caught in legal dilemmas, the Just War Theory becomes a grand international concern. An idea simply based on the criteria of justified means and justified ends (and intentions, of course), of which both are to an extent fixed into the 1949 Geneva Convention and the 1945 UN Charter, the two international treaties aiming still to govern – and civilize – the conduct of wars. Nevertheless, a just cyber war has difficulties peculiar to itself, which require almost continual checks. For, is it justifiable that a cyber attack could damage critical national infrastructures, if contemporary cyber incidents had not harmed civilians in any traditional sense, through bloodshed and violence? Relatedly, should they also take damage to private property and standards of living into account, and to what extent? Also, what harm can arise from the use of cyber sabotage as the first step of war, when it could result in far fewer, or no deaths at all? Indeed, what rules of engagement are constituted for a war that has hitherto taken place in the virtual dimension? For the most part, these questions have not yet been answered in the aforementioned treaties, notwithstanding their very significance to the conduct of modern warfare. (Though, at the same time, it would be wrong to assume that this task is easy.) Either way, it is evident that the existing laws, accustomed to physical violence, are enervated by the existence of so many 'holes,' and therefore less vigorous in the realm of cyberwarfare; but likewise because they are deprived in their 'ethical' use of that domain of war.

CONCLUDING REFLECTIONS ON
THE MODESTY OF CYBER LAW

As I have hitherto spoken collectively of the whole cybersecurity landscape, I must, therefore, if I reason consequentially, conclude that cyberspace is one of the grand challenges annexed to the lawmaker by its sheer breadth, unpredictability, recency, not to mention the want of empirical data (like major cyber incidents) in the records of the history of this new invention. To sum up what I have said in a few words – in the governance of cyberspace it is observable that national and international law, in point of argumentation, plainly adapted: restrains societal flaws that are reflected in the cyber domain; closes its many 'loopholes' that prevent it from becoming a prey to enervating cyber crimes; can check and balance the government's abuse of uncontrolled power; necessitates patience to fulfill its symbolic task of promoting the future welfare of its people; encourages and enforces prescriptive measures by which public and private cybersecurity is to get stronger; needs to address significant dilemmas in legal frameworks peculiar to war-making in order to maintain the 'civilized' conduct of war in cybersphere. Perhaps, as this little chapter has many reflections to recommend, I cannot silently pass over my contribution to the academic field, which, I think, has altered the theoretical and structural approach of addressing the issues by which cyberspace is pursued. It is also essential to bear in mind that the details of each legislation are, to some degree, dependent on each state by a concurrence of circumstances. But by allowing cyber law to bear an equal proportion between security with freedom, lawmakers should be incited to acquire constitutional dexterity in all its forms.

PART II

OVERSEEING THOSE WITH OVERSIGHT

INTRODUCTORY WORDS
AND PLAN OF THE WORK

I n a few years' time, admittedly, yet somewhat
anxiously, the world will have endured inside the
current security environment for three decades,
while terror attacks in the United Kingdom and
Europe,[67] foreshadow that this condition is unlikely
to change anytime soon. When the Cold War ended
abruptly and unexpectedly in 1991, a different kind
of threat – 'new terrorism' – was looming large cn
the horizon.[68] The September 11 attacks made this
very clear. Under a state of moral panic, therefore,
solutions were sought to prevent like events in the
future. The immediate response in the US was to rely
on their strongest weapon, military prowess, leading to the invasion of Afghanistan in October 2001,
to 'root out' the problem at its presumed source.
Domestically, on the other hand, it blamed the intelligence agencies for their failure to 'predict' and
'prevent,' setting off debates on the faults and weaknesses of the intelligence system.[69] In consequence,
the intelligence community in the United States was
reorganized, and legislation was passed to expand its
powers (for example, through the creation of the new
Department of Homeland Security or the Patriot
Act). Particularly, there was a notion that limitations

imposed on the agencies in the previous decades had undermined their effectiveness. The agencies had to be given free rein if they were to succeed in fulfilling their responsibilities. At least, that was the perception at the time. Little did they talk of intelligence oversight – which was not surprising, of course – given the characteristics of the new security threat.[70] While the threat in the Cold War was known, quantifiable and predictable – an entity with manifest boundaries – today's security threat appears to portray the exact opposite features.[71] It can hit from anywhere, at any time, and at anything.[72] Uncertainty is extraordinary. Targets for intelligence-gathering purposes are even more extraordinary. What lies ahead is indisputably a mammoth challenge for intelligence organizations, yet they cannot but confront it.

To fulfill this endeavor, intelligence agencies need information, the issue being, however, that not all information is openly and readily available.[73] Some are kept secret from prying eyes to maintain an advantage. Others are unknown and can never be known until they manifest themselves.[74] Intelligence agencies are not only aware of this fact, they also realize that they are not omnipresent entities; the minds that comprise its workforce are, after all, inescapably fallible. So stated, some believe that the solution lies in unleashing the powers of intelligence agencies in order to maximize their chances of alleviating that problem: torture and the use of intrusive surveillance capabilities being the two most extreme manifestations of this attitude.[75] Others, contrastingly, are outraged by such propositions, even rejecting the spying profession as a whole.[76] Notwithstanding, it would be almost inconceivable to do away with intelligence agencies altogether.[77] Under the stipulations of the social contract (at least within democratic societies),[78] citizens expect their respective governments to afford certain protection of their basic rights, from external and internal threats. Otherwise, the political cost would be irredeemable. Having argued thus, few would at the same time favor abandoning values that lie at the heart of democratic societies in exchange for security: leading to our third ethical approach, which attempts to bridge the gulf between the first two camps by a retreat to a reformulated Just War Theory, resulting in the Just Intelligence Theory and the consequent notions of *jus ad intelligentiam* (necessity) and *jus in intelligentia* (proportionality) as fundamental requirements before undertaking intelligence activities.[79]

Out of this school of thought has emerged, in turn, specific oversight mechanisms aimed at achieving a semblance of that balance in practice. Within the UK, for instance, we can witness the rise of the Intelligence and Security Committee (ISC), Judicial Commissioners, and the Investigatory Powers Tribunal, each responsible for overseeing particular aspects of the intelligence machinery.[80] Meanwhile, despite the fact that these have been criticized throughout the years by academics and government officials alike, only recently have they been reformed by the British Parliament: specifically, by the Justice and Security Act 2013, which reformed the ISC, and the Investigatory Powers Act 2016, which reformed the other two bodies. What is presently concerning, however, is that there have been very few scholarly assessments (in books and journal articles) of the performances and structural qualities of the aforementioned oversight bodies in the aftermath of those reforms. In relation to the ISC, the most recent writings merely offer brief assessments of the Committee,[81] while others are more or less restricted in their approach to assessing wider aspects of the Committee, focusing on narrower issues instead. With these issues in mind, it is essential that this lack of literature be addressed to find not only the weaknesses of the system, but also to offer a useful steppingstone towards improved structural reforms and oversight practices, all aimed at achieving a so-called 'just intelligence.'

As it has been a number of years since the reform of the Justice and Security Act 2013, the Intelligence and Security Committee's position offers the most appropriate option for assessing any oversight mechanism in the UK. So stated, the purpose of the last two chapters is twofold: first, to evaluate the Committee's performance in terms of its most recent activities, and second, to assess its structural strengths and weaknesses following the reforms of the Justice and Security Act 2013. Respectively, these will be examined in chapters six and seven. As there is still no consensus over the implications of oversight on intelligence effectiveness, the following chapter assesses the intelligence oversight versus intelligence effectiveness debate, concluding that oversight does not undermine intelligence effectiveness in its traditional sense, but rather improves it.

In undertaking this research paper, both primary and secondary sources have been examined.[82] Specifically, among the primary documents, a number of the annual, special, and press reports of the ISC are included; four acts of Parliament (Security Service Act 1989, Intelligences Service Act 1994, Justice and Security Act 2013 and Investigatory Powers Act 2016); a parliamentary briefing paper on the ISC; and a few news articles. With respect to secondary sources, it should be observed that although there has been significant literature on the topic of intelligence oversight in relation to the years before the Justice and Security Act 2013, an equally large dip in academic output since the passing of that act, as mentioned earlier, has largely taken away the opportunity for grounded debates throughout the final two chapters; though, this issue does not apply to the next chapter due to the breadth of its subject matter. It should be mentioned, at any rate, that the theoretical precedence set by existing literature offers a useful starting point, where relevant, for analyzing recent primary documents.

Here, a further methodological shortcoming must be confessed as well: the inherently secret nature of intelligence makes it difficult to know what exactly takes place within the so-called 'rings of secrecy.' Although there might not be a dearth of information in reality, a lack of key information could distort an accurate understanding of the overall picture.[83] So considered, even though the conclusions of this thesis are based on open information, it is also acknowledged that certain secret information may unavoidably undermine their validity or accuracy. Further methodological problems are specified in each individual chapter in consideration of any disparity between these three.

CHAPTER V

OF INTELLIGENCE OVERSIGHT
AND EFFECTIVENESS, WITH
THEIR DIFFERENCE

The history of intelligence oversight is the history of such facts, as the effects of the voluntary actions of people in civil society against the vices of tyranny, and it is, in many places, quoted to this day. And yet, until recently, very few showed any serious interest in the frame of their spy agencies generated from purely democratic principles, compared to the rest of the history of intelligence.[84] An observation on this difference presents the historical essence of the conduct of intelligence to our consideration: namely, by a sort of education, founded in the necessity to maintain certainty in the secure succession of the nation, progressively reduced and enforced by a set of taboos, which from time to time they received from their overseers.[85] The scheme of this education began to disintegrate in the mid-1970s, after a period of resentment provoked by the Watergate scandal, and alarmed into reflection by the promiscuous slaughter of the US intelligence community, under the pledged indulgence of Senator

Frank Church. Sooner or later, intelligence oversight menaced the public in the United Kingdom
and Canada, as in other countries. Yet, if there was
any increase of these oversight facilities, the want of
common consent manifested each in the degree of all
their description of oversight, without excluding the
principle of reverence to this political computation.
It is from this view of things that I will venture to
navigate this narrow, straitened discourse, to consider all those circumstances that demonstrate the
democratic ideas of freedom requires rather a more
robust form of legislative oversight, executed by their
committees, than at any time they may have authority or capacity to contrive. At present, I must content
myself with a discussion on this subject only, reserv-
ing for another time points wherein the oversight of
other mechanisms is concerned: consisting of various descriptions of controls and correctives included
in every sort of judicial, executory, organizational,
journalistic, societal, or international power.[86] Be
that as it may, I think some inquiries and observa-
tions on the work of legislative committees will still
be applicable to the other modes of vigilance.

In this choice of scope, our deliberations begin
with the arguments against oversight found in the act
of micromanagement or in destructive leaks. After a
course of attentive censure or qualification, I shall set
forth the positive impact of oversight in producing
accountable and effective intelligence in every one of
the democracies. A compelling opinion, the grounds
of which they ought to acknowledge.

DRAWBACKS OF OVERSIGHT

No difficulties occur in what has never been tried. I mean the consideration of the favourableness of insiders to all exertions against the cause of legislative oversight. In this, I may say of the breakthrough of one of the learned academicians of Intelligence Studies, Philip H. J. Davies, whose penetrating knowledge of the intelligence community concludes that executive oversight, standing on its own, provides for sufficient supervision of the agencies.[87] He finds that oversight bodies any other than the executive will not have the same degree of information and power upon these establishments, as some ministers of state who are among the approvers of their proceedings and operations; in other words, as he advances, when ministers are much inveterate in the professional and faculty habits of that narrow circle, they are rather qualified than disabled to administer the various external and internal interests which go to the formation of accountable intelligence processes. To this, he subjoins his 'triad' conditions: ministerial requirements and priorities, the authorization of royal warrants, and a fiscal leash – though all should be taken into consideration, nothing more than one is requisite for the success of such a plan as this.[88] After all, if the spy services were to circumnavigate the executive – all which turn them, as it were, into a species of institutional monster, called 'rogue elephants' – what is the power of external modes of oversight bodies, circumscribed and straitened by the immovable barriers of secrecy, to seek and dissolve the chaos of renegade elements of their own intelligence community? That is, the power of executive oversight, in its proper character, is indeed great, and long may it be able to preserve as long as its ministers are accountable to the legislature for the actions of their agencies – a question of another basis (or rather buttress) by which external relations may safely have recourse for their protection. In fact, it is expected that the demands they are to answer to the legislature are not easily avoidable. Having considered the composition of the British intelligence community as it stood in its original frame, to Davies it appears from the beginning that such a deputation as the Intelligence and Security Committee (ISC), in conjunction with the majority of the oversight channels, whilst it attempted to implement its creators' anticipated system of prescription, was already sufficient on its own, and therefore it does not have reason to presume upon future improvements of these proceedings.

It cannot, additionally, be denied that to some, guardians exterior to the executive appear in quite another point of view. Not being wholly read in the mazes of the *arcana* of the profession, and who do not understand those processes, they cannot but risk the leak of sources and methods of intelligence collection, or any other species of organizational capacity, both in the person presiding in it and in all their subordinates.[89] The critics, it is true, do suppose, perhaps impiously, that the temptation to derive political advantage is too strong for partisan committee members, I mean, the circumstance of the breach of secrecy which will serve most to blunt the reputation of their rival party, if not for good moral causes.[90] Time and resources are required to develop that union of means and sources which alone can produce all the good intelligence: such as to be capable of leading their interests to a defiance of their enemies, even though that leak of information, which makes an exposition of hints, will in some degree undermine these advantages, clearing the way for their enemies to develop countermeasures against these descriptions of intelligence collection. This idea of a ring of secrecy, confined to the least possible number of those who have access to information, is aimed at precluding the sore evil of a boundless circulation of private data.

Here is a second negative on the choice of the oversight. By way of a report on the influence of micromanagement, it is now assumed that the charge of watching over the operations of the intelligence community slows down the pace of the intelligence officials affected by it.[91] In this bureaucratic traffic, the personnel not only are to make provision for legal questions upon each and every decision at an operational level (though the able arrangement of intelligence operations requires the greatest skill and attention), but at any price they are to tenaciously adhere to the defining prescriptions and decisions of oversight institutions: besides those of their 'masters' (or ministers) who are enabled by their constitution. What is more, the recruits and current workforce know well that the idea of oversight furnishes a principle of sloth; the difficulties, through a labyrinth of confused detail, meet them in their course, and, in their opinion, the whole of their work becomes feeble, insecure and discouraging, if not absolutely disappointing.[92] It is this inability to wrestle with micromanagement which has obliged the leading advocates of effective intelligence to commence their scheme of reform with the abolition of some oversight mechanisms.

ANALYSIS OF THE PRECEDING DRAWBACKS

These sentiments may seem prevalent, but they are not without considerable faults and errors. For, considering the United Kingdom's highly coordinated and integrated intelligence community with their political masters, as well as its small size (say, compared to the United States), it would be surprising to find 'rogue' elements within the system anyway. With this in mind, what is really necessary are clear debates about the exact things intelligence agencies should or should not do. Phrased differently, 'how' and 'why' questions are better answered with the assistance of an outsider: a responsibility ideally provided through an oversight body external to the normal executive-agency circle. Needless to say, it should be acknowledged here that the political system plays a significant role in influencing differences between executive and legislative oversight mechanisms (in the United Kingdom, for instance, the executive as the majority party in the Houses of Parliament can greatly influence the latter). Certainly, this in itself appears to advocate the view that a better oversight system, generally speaking, requires a change in the political system. As this would be a far-fetched idea, however, one can only rely on alternatives, in this case, the current oversight mechanisms within the Houses of Parliament, in contrast to Davies' suggestions.

Second, though Davies' argument regarding ministerial accountability in our Palace of Westminster makes a compelling case in theory, it betrays credibility in practice. Specifically, the chief problem with Davies' contention is that ministerial accountability until the emergence of external oversight was almost non-existent, simply because intelligence, until then, was considered a taboo subject in Parliament: one that was left ideally under the purview of the Prime Minister and the executive generally speaking.[93] It was only with the development of oversight mechanisms inside the government (in the legislature and judiciary) that debates on intelligence matters gained momentum in official circles, while making it increasingly mainstream subject material. The overall point being, ministerial accountability to the House of Commons, as recognized by Davies, was more or less dormant until oversight mechanisms made official discussions of intelligence a regular activity.

So stated, it is now time to turn to our assessment of the second objection against intelligence oversight. From a quantitative point of view, as of May 2014, there had been a total of four ISC-related leaks.[94] Although these may seem very few at first sight, they can equally lead to damaging questions. Specifically, a crucial argument arising from this evidence would be that the four ISC leaks ultimately demonstrated any oversight committee is far from immune to prohibited disclosures, and that, because of this, the original suggestion to discontinue (or minimize) an oversight body's access to secret information is still an advisable recommendation. Though this may certainly be understandable on its own, it is nevertheless important to account for two qualitative aspects of the said leaks as well. First, it is not clear who disclosed them. In the final analysis, this makes blaming the Committee a difficult task. As for 'absent evidence,' there is little to show that the ISC was responsible for causing these disclosures. And, as Abram N. Shulsky and Gary J. Schmitt have pointed out, information can, in the general run of things, also be exposed by officials from within the executive who are incidentally in close contact with the committee oversight process (say, in handling and transporting documents).[95] That suggests, of course, that attention should be focused on the executive, in tightening restrictions – or reducing the number of members with access to secret information – rather than other information-gathering operatives. In turn, the second qualitative aspect is concerned with the fact that the said leaks did not damage national security in the first place; rather, they were mainly involved within the content of ISC reports immediately before their publication. In some ways, it may be stated that the harmless nature of the leaks, in themselves, offers a sense of reassurance for future cases, particularly if one is reminded of the fact that the majority of ISC members have been largely comprised of former senior officials inside the government, predominantly in such roles as Secretary of State for Defence, or Foreign and Commonwealth Affairs, who exhibit the necessary skills and experience in handling highly classified information, whilst fully understanding the implications of exposing sensitive material. Under those circumstances, all in all, when assessing the link between oversight and leaks, it may, in short, be argued that even though there is still uncertainty regarding the future of the ISC, it appears unlikely for committee members to irresponsibly expose information harmful to Britain's national security.

Lastly, it should be noted that the anxiety regarding micromanagement is, more or less, unfounded primarily due to the fact that oversight bodies are not supposed to interfere with operations at a tactical level. That is to say, they are not to 'control' operations but to 'supervise' them.[96] This, if reflected in practice, would mean almost no negative impact on intelligence effectiveness. Supervision, as will be demonstrated next, improves intelligence effectiveness. Furthermore, it is worth noting that there is little evidence in practice to substantiate the argument that micromanagement leads to ineffectiveness. To illustrate, the ISC, in pursuit of its mandate, can only 'review' intelligence operations, not 'oversee' them. In other words, the Committee can only examine the conduct of an intelligence operation retrospectively, but not during an operation. In another example, although one that lies outside the remit of the Committee, it may be useful to point out the authorization of certain 'urgent' operations which are undertaken by lower-level officials on behalf of the relevant

Secretaries of State and the Judicial Commissioner – both of which are currently required for authorizing almost all intelligence operations – which are then reviewed in the aftermath of those operations by those actors responsible to ensure right conduct according to their remit. With all this in mind, it may briefly be said that micromanagement should not be feared (as it usually is) by opponents of oversight, provided that suitable measures do exist to avoid unwanted ineffectiveness.

THE PROPER OBJECTS OF OVERSIGHT

Now that the criticisms against intelligence oversight have been assessed, it is time to delve into detailed reasons about the necessity and benefits of oversight. Broadly speaking, we examine the effect of intelligence oversight on two areas of intelligence: respectively, intelligence accountability and intelligence effectiveness. To start with, accountability, as a hallmark of democracy, is crucially about holding institutions or individuals responsible for their actions. At its core, therefore, lies a principal-actor relationship in which the actor is being held accountable to the principal. Democratic accountability would, in that sense, refer to 'people' as the principal and 'state' as the actor. Yet, as people are not readily available to perform as the principal, representatives are naturally elected to the legislature to fulfill that role instead. So, in this capacity, the legislature is, in theory, tasked to hold the executive (responsible for the state's governance) to account and prevent the potential abuse of power. These concepts noted, the same principle may also be applied to intelligence agencies – as institutions under the control of the executive – and the legislature. But what is required in this case is a mechanism that ensures secrecy and accountability at the same time: a task that is usually delegated to a parliamentary committee with authorized access to secret information, documents, and relevant personnel, without losing its status as an arm of the legislature.

It is with these thoughts in mind that intelligence agencies, as institutions of the executive, need, in principle, to be held accountable. The notion of 'checks and balances' lies, indeed, at the core of this argument. If the executive, in general, is held accountable at all times to prevent any abuse of its power, there is no reason for the intelligence community, which lies beneath it, to remain exempt from the system of 'checks and balances' either. Indeed, in any likening to George Orwell's dystopian police state in 1984,[97] intelligence agencies have the potential capabilities to 'foster a climate of suspicion and undermine trust [amidst citizens]' – at least in potential.[98] After all, men are not angels, as James Madison once stated; if men were angels, no government – or an oversight system, for that matter – would be necessary. It is only in authoritarian regimes that a system of 'checks and balances' – that is, democratic accountability – is not a requirement. The extent to which there is oversight of the intelligence community within a society, then, determines whether that society tends towards authoritarianism or democracy.[99]

Nonetheless, it must be said that holding intelligence agencies to account for their actions through oversight is not merely about promoting democratic values, but enhancing intelligence effectiveness at the same time: a significant benefit that is usually missed during heated debates about the importance of oversight for accountability. Stated so, one way in which this may occur is found in the effect of 'checks and balances' – in engendering some level of discipline and competitiveness in intelligence agencies. Certainly, if the agencies knew they were being watched by an external authority, they would be far more likely to fulfill their responsibilities effectively to avoid, say, scandals or public rebuke. Oversight, in this sense, would ensure that the agencies refine their techniques to achieve optimal performance. More importantly, they may likewise carry out their own investigations to identify failures and find solutions for correcting faults within the intelligence system.[100] Through this endeavor, they could particularly be useful in providing 'outsider' knowledge and exploring alternative methods that could potentially outperform traditional techniques. Indeed, it should be mentioned here that due to their place of origin, external oversight bodies are not intrinsically affected by 'groupthink' or other cognitive biases inherent in intelligence work. The investigation into the intelligence failure at the 7 July London bombings, for instance, recommended the establishment of a so-called 'devil's advocate' to encourage competitive analysis as a means to prevent similar failures in the future.[101] Everything considered, oversight not only discourages intelligence officials from acting poorly, it additionally effects systematic changes to faulty intelligence structures to help minimize flaws and, fundamentally, to refine the craft.

What is more, one should not ignore the fact that public support is indispensable to the work of intelligence agencies in democratic societies. To best demonstrate its relevance, it is clearly useful to refer to the British government's and intelligence agencies' wide-ranging efforts immediately following the Cold War to justify intelligence's continued existence – when questions were inevitably being asked by the public about the role and relevance of intelligence organizations in a world that had reached the 'end of history' (the victory of Western liberal democracy) or the perpetual 'peace dividend' (economic benefits derived from significant cuts to military spending).[102] Notable among these were, especially, the creation of a legal framework, which for the first time put agencies under a legal footing (outlining their functions and responsibilities openly to the public); public lectures by 'chiefs' within the various agencies, Dame Stella Rimington (former Director General of the Security Service) and Sir Colin McColl (Chief of the Secret Intelligence Service) in 1993, for instance, on the roles and responsibilities of the intelligence agencies, which, for all intents and purposes, was the first time any intelligence official had ever made a public appearance; not to mention the recent reforms, through the Justice and Security Act 2013 and the Investigatory Powers Act 2016 – all aiming to enhance transparency, whilst improving intelligence oversight powers. Each of these examples demonstrates, overall, that public opinion plays a crucial role in the work of the intelligence agencies. Moreover, it goes without saying that they are careful not to undermine that trust through questionable actions. The next thing to do now is to understand the rationale behind this influence. There are three aspects, generally speaking, which are worth noting.

The first is that if intelligence agencies aim to successfully expand their powers or finances and, more importantly, continue to exist, they would need to secure public support. If citizens are not convinced that taxpayer money is used justifiably, intelligence agencies are unlikely to have that support.[103] In turn, that reassurance is provided through oversight, a role that is fulfilled, above all, by improving transparency and, therefore, public understanding of intelligence affairs: reducing, thereby, misperceptions and distorted views (which are suffused with conspiracy theories and fiction) in the process, while pushing to the fore rather undistorted, 'center' (unbiased) views that neither underestimate, nor overestimate, intelligence capabilities. Briefly, then, it may be stated here that one reason why agencies cannot ignore public support is simply because their existence, powers and finances, for the most part, depend on public consent.

The second rationale for the significance of public opinion regarding intelligence effectiveness is the possibility of specific intelligence practices to alienate certain minorities within society – say, the Muslim minority – into radical acts of terror. One needs to be reminded here that in the struggle against fundamentalism, winning people's 'hearts and minds' remains the most crucial strategy. Engaging in controversial countermeasures undermines the potential to achieve that objective, essentially by diminishing the moral high ground over Islamic fundamentalism.[104] The role of oversight at a time of heightened security, then, would not only be to neutralize unnecessary security panics which result, essentially, in abusive and unchecked countermeasures, but also to condemn the use of such countermeasures as ineffective and damaging in the long-run or even the short-term.[105]

The third likely impact of public trust on intelligence agencies, in turn, would be to increase agencies' self-confidence, diminishing any previous self-doubt that might have resulted in uncertainty and, therefore, ineffectiveness.[106] If agencies know what they can, or cannot do, under the guidance of a strong oversight system, they would be more likely to make better decisions and implement them more effectively. On top of that, there would be little room for abiding intelligence agencies to order morally sensitive agents to undertake questionable activities with the end result of 'causing' an aggrieved member willing to put things right by 'blowing the whistle' and exposing the agency to public scandals and unhelpful media attention.

Apart from the significance of public support, however, it should be noted that oversight equally helps to hinder the politicization of intelligence. Politicization, briefly, refers to an unhealthy relationship between policymakers (consumers of intelligence) and intelligence professionals (producers of intelligence). Politicization occurs when the former essentially encourages the latter, directly or indirectly, to support predetermined policies: directly – whereby policymakers select only those bits of intelligence that favor their policies; indirectly – wherein political currents at the time (in a sense) manipulate intelligence officials themselves into providing biased information. In both cases, then, intelligence is used not objectively to shape policy decisions, but in a biased manner to serve existing preconceptions. Certainly, the intelligence on Iraqi weapons of mass destruction is a prominent case in point in its demonstration of how policymakers attempted to gain public support by disclosing misleading intelligence. Nevertheless, it is important to remember that some degree of politicization is crucial for ensuring that intelligence remains relevant. Without specific targets set by policymakers, intelligence runs the risk of becoming irrelevant and, therefore, ineffective. The role of oversight, under this context, essentially is to keep a 'close eye' on this government-agency relationship to ensure that it becomes neither politicized nor irrelevant by observing and identifying misbalances within the system or areas that are not properly overseen.

THE FUTURE OF OVERSIGHT,
AND DIFFERENCES OF BEARING

Notwithstanding the benefits gained from intelligence oversight, as demonstrated in the previous sections, it is unlikely that the present perception of oversight will lose its influence over policymakers and intelligence officials any time soon. This may be explained by the underlying factor that intelligence agencies were, after all, established and developed out of a mindset heavily shaped by 'realism,' which suggests, ultimately, that national self-interest in an anarchic world (that lacks an all-encompassing supranational authority to prevent the likelihood of conflict between nations) lies at the core of all international relations. Under these circumstances, nations are responsible for their own security, and intelligence is one way how security may be guarded. Indeed, the struggle between the intelligence agencies of the West and their counterparts in the communist world during the Cold War made sure this mindset was 'hardwired' into their organizational outlook. From that perspective, it would have been considered inept if the agencies were to relinquish their special powers when the enemy operated without restraint.

In response to these statements, one particularly wonders about the future of intelligence agencies: Can their 'realist' outlook be altered in practice, and how? It is clearly evident that changes have, indeed, transpired in the aftermath of the Cold War, with the development of transnational terrorism as the new threat. In particular, there has been an obvious trend towards increasing collaboration with international partners, mainly to compensate for one another's limitations. To effectively counter terror threats from Al-Qaeda, or Daesh, for example, Western intelligence agencies require human sources on the ground infiltrating terrorist cells and so forth. Yet, one of the more significant weaknesses of Western intelligence agencies currently is that they lack ethnic diversity in the workforce, when this factor is so highly crucial for countering threats that originate in other parts of the world (markedly the Middle East). To compensate for this weakness, then, they collaborate with the relevant intelligence agencies in the region, whom, in exchange for certain benefits from the West, offer information gained from their human sources. Ultimately, these changes to traditional ways of undertaking intelligence demonstrate that there is, indeed, a possibility for altering the outlook of the agencies to voluntarily embrace oversight. This will not, however, be an easy task to achieve, and trust will be essential in fulfilling that endeavor.

There is still a widespread notion that oversight merely aims to ensure accountability – as a matter of principle only – and apart from that, it harms intelligence effectiveness. But as was argued in this chapter, not only are there significant issues with the three criticisms against intelligence oversight (futility of oversight, leaks, and micromanagement), it was argued at the same time that intelligence oversight improves intelligence effectiveness through a combination of strengthening the morale and focus of intelligence officials and organizations, refining intelligence techniques, ensuring public trust and precluding the politicization of intelligence. In doing so, this chapter contributed to academic literature in two specific areas: first, in critiquing Davies' argument regarding the futility of oversight, and second in suggesting the core reasons behind the agencies' perception of intelligence oversight, as shown in the last section. With those in mind, the more appropriate task now is to assess how intelligence oversight performs in the United Kingdom. The Intelligence and Security Committee, as a central oversight mechanism within the British intelligence machinery, is an appropriate place to start.

CHAPTER VI

REFLECTIONS ON THE OVERSIGHT OF THE
INTELLIGENCE AND SECURITY COMMITTEE

As a central oversight mechanism over the intelligence machinery, an effective parliamentary committee is crucial. The aim of this chapter is to assess whether this role is being fulfilled satisfactorily by the Intelligence and Security Committee (ISC) based on its efforts, initiated in March 2015, when it published a report on women in the intelligence community.[107] It is worth mentioning there is, presently, no academic literature that systematically assesses the ISC's efforts then. For this reason, our analysis in this chapter is based on primary official documents. Overall, in assessing the Committee's performance, two criteria are identified. The first determines the Committee's influence on reforming the intelligence community. The next subsequently evaluates the Committee's contribution to transparency. It is important to point out here that this chapter does not assess solely the work of the Committee, chaired by Dominic Grieve, from September 2015 until May 2017. Rather, it takes into account the work of the previous term chaired by Sir Malcolm Rifkind. This is simply because the work of each term is carried out by their successors. Furthermore, it should be mentioned at the outset that this chapter does not in any way intend to evaluate the ethics behind the Committee's statements and conclusions.

Before continuing, a methodological issue needs to be addressed. At first sight, it may seem that assessing merely two criteria is insufficient. This, however, is unavoidable mainly because other possible approaches for assessing the performance of the ISC are largely irrelevant and unnecessary. A key example that comes to mind is Peter Gill's quantitative analysis of the ISC.[108] Specifically, his analysis consists of calculating the number of paragraphs within the Committee reports to gain insight into their general output. In his article, he concluded that there was a clear rise in the number of paragraphs produced in the reports. Notwithstanding, such an approach to the Committee's efforts from 2010 would now be unnecessary, largely because the current context is drastically different from that period within which Peter Gill's article was published. At the time, specifically, there was suspicion that the Committee produced reports not really aiming to contribute to genuine oversight, but merely to tick boxes as an oversight body tasked with a number of responsibilities; in some ways, this perception was reinforced by the Committee's first few reports within which, for the most part, documentation proved relatively brief and rudimentary. With that in mind, the central reason why this methodology is now unsuitable is largely due to the fact that suspicions about the Committee do not truly apply to it (in itself) anymore: or at least not from that angle (essentially), because it has – so far – produced significant output consistently throughout the years. Henceforth, what needs to be questioned now is not whether the Committee is doing any work at all quantitatively, but whether its reports are qualitatively meaningful. It is vital for this reason that this chapter intends to solely evaluate the Committee's performance based on its qualitative output, not its quantitative output.

HOW TO JUDGE THE PROPER INFLUENCE OF THE ISC

In assessing performance, the ISC's influence on the way intelligence activities are undertaken, or the sort of reforms implemented through policies, are important criteria to consider. Dialogue, not monologue, is essential if oversight is to have any significance in practice. As stated, to assess the ISC's influence, this section focuses solely on the Committee's influence in two separate areas: firstly, the Investigatory Powers Act 2016 and, secondly, women in the UK intelligence community. The primary reason for choosing the two areas, basically, is because out of all the Committee's reports on various topics, within this time period, the government had issued 'responses' only in these two areas: all meaning that the Committee's other activity, on the UK Drone Strikes in Syria, would have to be excluded from the assessment. It is worth mentioning that government responses are important tools for assessing the Committee's efficacy mainly because they provide an overview of what has been achieved and what is planned to be achieved – in response to the Committee's original reports. Without a government response on the Committee's UK Drone Strikes in Syria report, the present task of assessing its performance would be nearly impossible: not only because there are no relevant official or press statements on the matter, but equally because the secrecy involved in intelligence precludes any sort of glitter into that shadowy world. Admittedly, the same problem also applies to areas wherein the government has responded to perceived concerns – for without any insight behind closed doors, it would not be possible to ascertain whether the government, or the agencies, did implement the accepted recommendations in reality.

THE WOMEN OF THE UK
INTELLIGENCE COMMUNITY

To start with the report on women in the intelligence community, the governmental response to that document made it explicitly clear the three main agencies, the Secret Intelligence Service (MI6), the Security Service (MI5), and Government Communications Headquarters (GCHQ), were making obvious progress in developing gender equality, recounted some evidence of what each agency had done before the publication of the response and what they planned to do in the future. Certainly, it should be mentioned here that up until the publication of the report, there was, nonetheless, general agreement over the need to attain gender diversity among the agencies. Although this may raise questions about the value of the ISC report, it may starkly be pointed out that the ISC substantially contributed to its development by identifying specific faults and solutions that the agencies could themselves identify to improve short-comings in that aspect of their organizations. On the whole, the Committee's investigations indicated that, broadly speaking, the agencies were lacking in six areas: the targeting of 'other' groups of women for recruitment (women or mothers in middle age, or mid-career, who may not be university graduates), career management (to encourage women to think strategically about their careers for, say, promotion), setting up informal support networks (for network-ing opportunities, or sharing experiences), women limited to certain jobs (in human resources, for in-stance, after receiving maternity leave), international connections (to share experiences and best practice), and tackling the 'permafrost' (deeper cultural and behavioral issues).

According to the response, both the govern-ment and the agencies 'wholeheartedly' agreed with the ISC regarding the significance of diversity for intelligence effectiveness in addition to legal and eth-ical reasons. Overall, the response demonstrated im-provements could be made in the six aforementioned areas, offering evidence for each in turn. Gender di-versity, for instance, appeared to have improved from both a quantitative and qualitative perspective in the 14-month gap between the publication of the actual report and the government response – demonstrated, for example, by the five percent increase in female recruits in MI5; an increasing focus on 'emotional intelligence,' for eligibility requirements in recruiting, as opposed to the standard qualifications (university degrees); increasing assistance to women in moving up the career ladder to senior positions (for instance, through GCHQ's Career Portal, created to assist women in planning their careers); or, more prominently, reaching their 'highest ever positions [all three agencies] in the Stonewall top employer's workplace equality index.' Notwithstanding, it must be stated here that in spite of the obvious progress made by the three organizations in 14 months, an assessment of the Committee's influence in the long-term (at the moment) is too soon, and made particularly difficult, as was earlier mentioned, by the fact that there is no possible insight into the secretive organization of the agencies apart from information made public by the Committee, which dissolved in May 2017 before the general elections, the government or chiefs of the agencies; scandals, on the other hand, would be highly unlikely to address gender diversity in the intelligence community. Those being stated, though it may be argued that a longer-term assessment of the Committee's influence in this area is not currently possible, it is apparent that the Committee has had an obvious short-term influence on the government. It, thus, remains for the future members of the Committee to assess whether the agencies have achieved enough. In any event, we may also add here that the agencies did achieve what the Committee itself had precisely required it to achieve: that is, to significantly demonstrate 'progress' in the six areas that were noted earlier.

DRAFT INVESTIGATORY POWERS BILL

Having considered the Committee's influence on the outcome of their report concerning women in the intelligence community, it is now time to turn to the Committee's other report on the Investigatory Powers Act 2016. In the aftermath of Snowdon's revelations, there was widespread public suspicion regarding intrusive intelligence capabilities. Under that context, the objective of the Investigatory Powers Act 2016 was, primarily, to transform the law on the agencies' use and oversight of 'investigatory' (or, simply, intrusive!) powers. In doing so, three parliamentary committees scrutinized the bill and offered recommendations to improve the legislation. In addition to the ISC, the other committees were the Joint Committee and the House of Commons Science and Technology Committee, each with their own specific agenda, and at times overlapping recommendations, some of which were subsequently implemented by the government. Therefore, to determine the ISC's influence on such a crucial area, an assessment of the extent to which the government implemented the Committee's recommendations is needed.

In its report on the draft Investigatory Powers Bill, the ISC altogether made 22 recommendations. Out of these, only seven – approximately 36 percent, or a bit more than a third – were wholly accepted by the executive. Out of the remaining twelve, ten were rejected, and five were partially accepted. From a quantitative point of view, it may be suggested that in influencing the Investigatory Powers Bill, the Committee was successful only to a limited extent. Pinpointing the reasons behind successful recommendations, however, is difficult. It may be the case, for instance, that while some recommendations were too sensitive to be ignored by the executive – such as recommendation ix, which advised that the 'security and intelligence agencies must apply for a new BPD [bulk personal datasets] warrant [...] if they wish to continue to retain or examine any of the material obtained from a BPD warrant that has not been renewed, or is [canceled]' – others appeared to be neglected weaknesses that did not require significant compromise on the part of the government – including, for instance, recommendation x, to clarify the definition of 'technical capability' regulations. Examining overlapping recommendations, in turn, seems to suggest that these were largely chosen because of the influence of two committees on a single issue. Hence, four out of five partially accepted recommendations were also overlapping recommendations with the Joint Committee. What is particularly noteworthy in these responses is that the government seemed particularly to favor the recommendations of the Joint Committee more than the ISC's: hence the reason why for their partial acceptance. One clear example, of course, is recommendation v which suggested, 'Reducing the period of time within which urgent warrants must be reviewed by a judge' to two days compared to the Joint Committee's three days in recommendation 36, which was accepted instead. With respect to rejected recommendations, on the other hand, it should be stated that the reasons behind them are more difficult to pinpoint because of the lack of insight into the government's decision-making process. Specifically, it is almost impossible to say whether a government response is truly genuine in its criticism of a recommendation or merely protective of the agencies' powers. Of course, to answer that question would be an almost impossible task without any access to the 'rings of secrecy' in question. All considered, these seem to suggest that a more accurate representation of the Committee's role in influencing policies is that the government rather treated the Committee as a body that offered supplementary recommendations alongside those of two other committees, the Joint Committee and the House of Commons Science and Technology Committee and that the government more or less picked and chose the recommendations it found useful.

TRANSPARENCY

Those themes being said and done, the next criteria in assessing the Committee's performance concerns its contribution to transparency, mainly, as we need to be reminded here, because one of the Committee's most important responsibilities – apart from improving public understanding of intelligence activities and organizations, is also to raise the awareness and expertise of parliamentarians in matters of intelligence. Needless to say, among all oversight mechanisms, civil oversight (in society) is usually considered the most influential due to its ability to demand reform from the government. And as such, it is vital that this responsibility be realized as best as possible. Transparency is, after all, a hallmark of democracy. Regardless, there are, generally speaking, two ways within which the ISC's contribution to transparency may be assessed: the first is based on the actual content of its reports, and the second how accessible they are to the general public. While the first is concerned with the range and depth of issues (important or otherwise) reported by the Committee, the latter is more concerned with their readability by members of the general public. Notably, it is worth mentioning that a third criterion would be to assess the actual effect of the Committee's output on public knowledge, as well as parliamentary expertise. This would currently be an almost impossible task, however, as it requires research on a comprehensive scale, say in particular, through qualitative and quantitative surveys, which presently do not exist.

In order to assess the ISC's contribution to transparency through the actual content of its reports, it is perhaps best to start with the Committee's most important work in recent years on the issue of digital privacy and surveillance, instigated by the widespread controversy that arose out of Snowden's revelations: that is to say, the Committee's findings on privacy and security.[109] In short, the ISC report's most important contribution to transparency was in outlining what intrusive capabilities were exactly available to the British intelligence agencies – GCHQ as well as MI5 and MI6 – and, for that matter, what oversight mechanisms there were to preclude any abuse of their powers against civil liberties. Overall, the report was significant because it sought to enhance oversight on a highly controversial area inside the field of intelligence by improving transparency and public knowledge of the matter. What is additionally noteworthy is that it was the first official report in the country to detail what previously had been kept secret about intelligence capabilities from the public.[110] The Committee even stated that the report disclosed for the first time an intrusive capability hitherto unknown to the public, that is, the 'bulk personal datasets,' which, as it happened, was not alluded to, in its literal sense, in official circles. Admittedly, though much information was doubtless 'redacted' from the report on bulk personal datasets due to some of the material's supposed sensitivity to national security, the report did outline what that capability was and how it was being conducted.

Certainly, while it may be maintained that the majority of the capabilities examined in the report were known to the public beforehand, it should nevertheless be acknowledged that the report's chief contribution was in providing an insider's peek into intelligence processes that are usually misinterpreted by outsiders. Particularly, this was evident when following Snowdon's revelations. It was alleged, after all, that GCHQ had 'mass surveillance' capabilities. Usually, in particular, GCHQ was likened to an all-seeing eye that represented a would-be instrument of the Big Brother state in George Orwell's dystopian *Nineteen Eighty-Four*. This misperception was made even clearer, however, when the Committee's report precisely explained how GCHQ conducted information-gathering and what it could access in reality according to its actual capabilities. Indeed, as the report expounded, GCHQ can only analyze 'a very small percentage of the bearers,' and that, out of this, only a certain amount is retrieved following selection and filtering.[111] In explaining the various processes behind the agencies' capabilities, the report furthermore clarified, as well as highlighted, the weaknesses of ambiguous terminologies, such as communications data, or the differences between bulk, class, or thematic intrusion. With those in mind, the clarity offered by the document essentially cleared the sensationalism encompassing the intrusive capabilities of the British intelligence agencies. Of course, this was helped by the credibility of the Committee as having access to secret information.

As was earlier mentioned, alongside an overview of Britain's intrusive intelligence capabilities, the report equally outlined the oversight mechanisms and limitations hindering any abuse of power, particularly describing, for example, the implications of the Human Rights Act 1998, authorization of different types intelligence operations (say, international, or domestic, urgent, or otherwise) and the different types of warrants involved, not to mention other oversight mechanisms undertaken by the Commissioners and the Tribunal, amongst others. In this regard, the most noteworthy feature of the report was that it drew together safeguards against any violation of civil liberties, oversight mechanisms, and the legal limitations imposed on the agency from several scattered acts of Parliament (for instance, the Police Act 1997, Justice and Security Act 2013, Regulation of Investigatory Powers Act 2000) into a single, coherent and clear document – doubtless, a measure that was specifically required at the time for enhancing transparency.

These noted, it should additionally be pointed out that apart from its work on privacy, the Committee's other endeavors have extended to other significant areas such as the UK Lethal Drone Strikes in Syria report in 2015 or 'detainee mistreatment and rendition' (in another report) – both of which address issues of great significance to the public – as well as less controversial, but equally important, areas such as the administration and policies of the agencies in relation, for example, to diversity and women in the workplace. Although it should be said that the breadth and detail of the ISC's investigations so far are commendable, indeed, it is disappointing to find that the Committee is yet to investigate perhaps one of the most problematic issues within intelligence: outsourcing or the privatization of intelligence. This is particularly surprising considering not only the increasing rise of outsourcing since September 11, but at the same time, the remarkably limited oversight over the private sector, which inevitably raises questions about the likelihood of private actors carrying out unacceptable actions. Certainly, even though it may be argued that the size of intelligence within the private sector in the UK is nowhere near as large as that of America's, there are, nevertheless, enough activities to require some degree of attention. Evidently, a number of UK-based private intelligence companies presently include National Security Strategic Investment Fund, Control Risks and Aegis Defence Services, amongst others. Whether a scandal is required to push the Committee to investigate this area inside intelligence remains to be seen. It is, however, clear that if the Committee aims to further its credibility as an oversight body that promotes transparency, it will need to investigate the outsourcing of intelligence in the UK sooner, rather than later.

THE SENSE OF ACCESSIBILITY AND INACCESSIBILITY

Apart from the ISC's contribution to transparency through content, credit must additionally be given to the Committee's efforts to facilitate the accessibility of their work for public education. After all, if reports cannot be communicated to the people, then it is unlikely that the Committee's reports, which intend to enhance transparency, above all, would have any impact on public perception. So considered, one of the Committee's useful tools for enhancing accessibility is found in its press statements, which are released either when specific reports are published (to provide brief summaries) or when a scandal of some sort demands that the Committee provide an impartial insider's perspective. Notably, these are always brief, succinct, and stylistically far more readable than the Committee's longer reports, while the fact that the media sets these up for the consumption of the general public suggests that they are likely to be within the ordinary citizen's reach. To illustrate, the Committee's press statement in response to a scandal was with regard to allegations that GCHQ had been tasked by the former American President, Barack Obama, to 'wiretap' the 2016 US presidential election candidate, Donald Trump. In its statement, the Committee was clear that the allegations were false. Following the release of that statement, media outlets of various types started to publish the Committee's response in their news articles.[112]

Nonetheless, there is an important criticism respecting the accessibility of Committee reports. It is worth noting that accessible reports are more important for providing a detailed understanding of intelligence issues, as opposed to the mere broad brushstrokes of press statements. The issue, however, is that reports are, for the most part, unlike press releases in terms of their accessibility; they follow an unfriendly rigid style and structure, which essentially erodes their public accessibility. In spite of that, the only report in all of the Committee's history that has not followed this pattern is the Committee's report on women in the intelligence community, examined earlier. The report is particularly unique for producing a friendly style and format as well as useful diagrams and tables – similar in some ways to a booklet, not a legislative document – which all facilitate understanding of the material. At the same time, what is particularly noteworthy is that the report does not tend towards sensationalism either. Regardless, the fact that this way of writing has not been repeated since then is a source of regret. It would be recommended that the Committee returns to that format in future reports.

To conclude, perhaps one of the more surprising facts about the current literature on Britain's Intelligence and Security Committee is the lack of a systematic work that solely assesses the Committee's performance, rather than its structures. The consequence is that the literature has been almost devoid of any theoretical framework with clear boundaries. Through an investigation of such theoretical boundaries, two specific criteria were identified for the purposes of the ISC: influence and transparency. Subsequently, the limitations of those criteria were demonstrated by incorporating particular methodological problems found in the study of intelligence. The resulting outcome then allowed for an assessment of the Committee's recent performance. It was concluded that in both transparency and influence, the Committee demonstrated a mixed performance. Though that, in itself, may have offered an indication as to what the Committee could do to improve upon its shortcomings in the future, the next research topic to address would be on assessing the structural qualities that influence the Committee's output in the first place. This task will be addressed in the next chapter.

CHAPTER VII

THOUGHTS ON THE STRUCTURAL STRENGTHS AND WEAKNESSES OF THE INTELLIGENCE AND SECURITY COMMITTEE

Notwithstanding heavy criticism, from academics and others, of the powers and capabilities of the Intelligence and Security Committee (ISC) from its overall establishment in 1994, it nearly took two decades before the Committee's structure was reformed by the Justice and Security Act 2013. Despite that reform, however, there is yet to be a systematic assessment of the Committee's reformed structure within scholarship. The objective of this chapter, accordingly, is not only to address that lack of literature, but also to set the stage for improved policymaking in relation to the Committee's structure. While primary documents are used to obtain up-to-date information about the Committee's current structure and state of affairs, secondary texts are similarly used, where applicable, for their grounded approach in addressing the relevant issues. On the whole, this chapter is divided into five sections. Each section assesses a single structural property of the Committee. Respectively, these comprise membership, reporting, mandate, access to information, and political will. Yet, when all is said and done, it is concluded that the Justice and Security Act 2013 failed to accommodate the Committee's most crucial weakness, incomplete access to information, though it also admits that the reform did raise the Committee's potential to achieve far-reaching powers and capabilities. It is important to note here that the main purpose of this chapter is to assess strengths and weaknesses inside an oversight body's structure, not to identify solutions for it. Where solutions are mentioned, the purpose merely is to offer ideas for possible future reforms of the Committee.

Before going any further, two methodological details must be mentioned. First, in assessing structural qualities of the ISC, it is notable that there is no ideal framework in practice that could be used as a standard. Instead, what we are left with are, as Amy Zegart rightly has testified, weaknesses that we use as our starting point to reach a hypothetical ideal.[113] This approach is, unavoidably, adapted for the purposes of this chapter. Second, alongside the five aforementioned criteria, one may also include a further criterion based on 'staff and resources.' This decision was not made, however, because in almost all cases, there appears to be a single outcome to an assessment of that criteria: simply, more staff and resources are required. As this is a valid point presently with the Committee (not to mention the fact it is very likely going to be in the near future), there seems no need for a detailed scrutiny of that criterion in this chapter. Rather, the aim solely has been to focus on those areas which are more, or less, disputable.

THE PROPRIETY OF MEMBERSHIP

The importance of membership, first and foremost, lies with the fact that it determines the Committee's independence from the executive. If the executive were to appoint members, the Committee's decisions would be, ultimately, suspiciously viewed because of their likelihood to favor intelligence agencies and government policies, especially if they were from the majority party (executive). As bodies that are tasked to oversee the intelligence community on behalf of the people and uphold accountability in consequence, this would be considered inappropriate. An effective membership selection process should, then, take this into account. So stated, this was indeed the case prior to the Justice and Security Act 2013. At the time, ISC members and its chairman were appointed by the Prime Minister (PM) after consultation with the Leader of the Opposition. Inevitably, this had resulted in widespread controversy regarding the independence of the Committee. The most significant consequence of that controversy was the passing of the Justice and Security Act 2013. With the passing of that act, the task of appointing Committee members was transferred from the PM to Parliament, though the PM still needed to nominate members in consultation with the Opposition Leader. Whether that reform resolved the controversy over the independence of the Committee, however, may still be questioned. In particular, it may be argued that since the PM can still nominate members, the Committee is not, as a matter of fact, truly independent. This was the view suggested by David Davis in 2015 in rebuking the endeavors of the Committee.[114]

Nevertheless, there are two possible counterarguments in response to this view. The first was offered by Sir Malcolm Rifkind (former chairman of the Committee), who highlighted the isc's actual composition, made up of a 'cross-party group of mps and peers,' to remind Davis that the Committee was not in reality singularly dominated by the majority party. The second counterargument, in turn, is that in spite of the pm's ability to nominate, Parliament nevertheless has the final say on who may be appointed at the end of the day. That, in turn, could have the benefit of striking an appropriate balance between independence and some level of trust between the executive and the Committee.

In assessing the first counterargument, although evidence appears to support Rifkind's statement (regarding the 'cross-party' nature of the Committee), it also appears that the Justice and Security Act 2013 has not really had a fundamental impact on the composition of the Committee since it was passed. This is, in particular, demonstrated by the fact that the composition of the Committee, more or less, remained similar after the passing of that act – namely, four Conservative, three Labour, one Crossbench, and one Scottish National Party – when the Committee dissolved in May 2017, compared to four Conservative, three Labour, one Liberal Democrat and one Crossbench in July 2012 – suggesting perhaps that before the passing of the act, there was already an expectation for more balanced 'cross-party' committees (that roughly reflected the composition of Parliament).

The main issue with that problem, however, is that there are, in reality, two other issues more urgent than the chairmanship of the Committee. The first weakness, specifically, concerns the slow appointment of members to the Committee. Since the beginning of May 2017, for instance, when the term dissolved, no members had yet been appointed to the ISC until November 2017. As Andrew Defty noted, a similar period of inactivity also occurred from February 2015, when Rifkind resigned from his post as Chairman, until, essentially, September 2015 when the new Committee was appointed following the May 2015 general elections.[115] Taking all those into account, it remains the case that the UK had been, for almost a period of 12 months, without a parliamentary intelligence oversight committee, in negligence of Chairman Dominic Grieve's statement that 'it is not in the public interest for oversight of the intelligence community to be left unattended for any period of time.' What these comments indicate, overall, is that there is a clear weakness in terms of appointing Committee members in a timely fashion and that serious consideration must be given to finding a solution.

On top of that, a further weakness requiring urgent attention concerns the expertise and experience of the Committee members within the field of intelligence, primarily because the complexity (and 'steep learning curve') of intelligence matters would preclude inexperienced members from fulfilling their responsibilities effectively, requiring them instead to remain in their post for several years before they become proficient at oversight.[116] That, clearly, asks for a certain degree of continuity in the appointment of members, one that was surely applied consistently within the UK since the establishment of the ISC. In spite of that fact, the issue of expertise has now become particularly important because, as Andrew Defty pointed out in his commentary for the Royal United Services Institute (RUSI), the members 'appointed in 2015 [were] the most inexperienced since the ISC was first established in 1994.' Amongst all its members, 'only two had served for the whole of the previous parliament.' Defty observed, additionally, that for the next term, 'even if all the remaining members are reappointed [...], only one, Lord Lothian, will have more than two years' experience on the committee.' Needless to say, this indicates that such committees are likely to still be inexperienced, not unlike the previous terms. This can especially be an issue if they were to continue the work of their predecessors. Essentially, they would be unable to 'take off,' as it were, when they landed in their posts. Certainly, then, there is a clear need to find possible solutions to that problem. What these could be, however, is currently difficult to answer, especially if the answer largely depends on members rather than the Committee structure. One possible solution would be to adopt a similar system to the Canadian Security Intelligence Review Committee, as an external review body comprised of non-parliamentary experts within the field of intelligence. As this is unlikely to occur in the UK, other solutions need to be reflectively sought.

REPORTING

Alongside membership, reporting is likewise significant for ensuring independence from the executive. After all, one of the ISC's responsibilities is to produce annual and other reports for policymakers and the public. When reports are published through the Prime Minster, what becomes public is essentially determined by the executive, since the executive will have the power to detract information on the grounds of national security – even if national security may not be the actual reason – thus diminishing transparency. One of the changes brought about as a result of the Justice and Security Act 2013 was that the ISC is now allowed to report directly to Parliament following consultation with the executive. What ensued, in consequence, was that the Committee had the option to negotiate with, rather than submit to the will of, the executive and the agencies when it came to allowing public access to 'redacted' parts of its reports. In this sense, the Committee had the power to strengthen transparency by making independent decisions about its reporting process. In contrast to the period prior to the Justice and Security Act 2013, this certainly appeared to be a significant improvement.

In spite of that statement, however, it is difficult to say whether the reform has had a positive outcome in practice. This is because even though the Committee may now have the option to submit its reports to Parliament directly, bypassing the executive in the process, it is unlikely that it would do so. This is for the important reason that it needs to be trusted by the executive or the agencies (to some extent, at least) if it is to gain access to secret information. More disappointing, however, is that there appear to be few, if any, alternatives to this reporting system. The only way to remove the focal reason behind its weak independence in relation to the executive and the agencies would be to give the Committee complete access to secret information – removing, in consequence, its need for trust and cooperation with the executive and the agencies. All things considered, though the Committee's reporting system appears to guarantee effective oversight on paper, a closer examination of the system in practice indicates that there is still room for improvement. Though there may appear to be no alternatives to the actual reporting structure itself, structural reform of the Committee (in terms of full access to information) may prove to be the solution.

MANDATE

Either way, assessing the Committee's mandate is also significant as it determines what a parliamentary committee can and cannot do. When the ISC was established by the Intelligence Services Act 1994, it was tasked to oversee the 'expenditure, administration and policy' of the three main intelligence agencies, MI6, MI5, and GCHQ. What is more, it was given the authority to initiate its own inquiries on any matter that fell under its mandate. The government did not, in this sense, determine which investigations it needed to undertake. With the passing of the Justice and Security Act 2013, the Committee's mandate expanded to include 'operations,' and others agreed in a 'memorandum of understanding' with the Prime Minister – of not only the three aforementioned intelligence agencies, but also the various arms in the wider intelligence community, namely the Joint Intelligence Committee (JIC), Office for Security and Counter-Terrorism, National Security Secretariat, Defence Intelligence, and Assessments Staff. These improvements to the Committee's structure were un-doubtedly welcome: it could oversee not only wider aspects of the agencies' activities, but additionally the work of the wider intelligence community. The Committee's new-found ability to oversee 'opera-tions,' in particular, was significant for it allowed it to look beyond more 'managerial' issues – in regard to the administration or expenditure of the agencies – into an area which was bound to enhance its ability to critique policies and agencies' activities.

These are not to say, however, that the Committee's mandate has reached an ideal stage. There is, in fact, a crucial weakness that must be taken into account, one that arises mainly out of its inability to gain access to all classified information. To expand on this point, it is first important to set out the three conditions required for undertaking investigations into the 'operations' of the agencies. These are dictated in the Justice and Security Act 2013 in the following way: 'the ISC and the Prime Minister are satisfied that the matter is not part of any ongoing intelligence or security operation, and [...] is of significant national interest;' 'the Prime Minister has asked the ISC to consider the matter;' or 'the ISC's consideration of the matter is limited to the consideration of information provided voluntarily to the ISC [either at the Committee's request or not]' by the three main agencies or a government department – it is worth noting that only one of these conditions is required before the Committee can investigate an 'operation.' Admittedly, it seems clear that the second and third conditions do not raise any particular doubt about the Committee's ability to trigger investigations; the executive or the agencies, after all, undertake work on behalf of the Committee to initiate investigations. Yet, the main issue is in relation to the first condition. Specifically, if the Committee is to initiate an investigation into a particular aspect of the intelligence community, it first needs to be aware of the existence of that aspect – of an 'unknown unknown,' in other words. Without that knowledge, the Committee would be unable to question controversial practices on the part of the agencies. It would remain in the dark unless a whistleblower or otherwise revealed its existence. What these factors indicate, overall, is that although the current mandate system may theoretically be suitable for effective oversight, the Committee's lack of complete access to information hinders the optimal use of this authority in practice.

Before examining the next criteria, a further criticism against the current mandate system should be pointed out as well. Specifically, it may be argued that the Committee's inability to oversee operations proactively (before or during an operation), by virtue of the first aforementioned condition – that is, 'that the matter is not part of any ongoing intelligence or security operation' – could undermine its ability to prevent inappropriate intelligence practices before they occur. Yet, there are two problems in adopting this approach. The first problem is that a continuous proactive approach is likely to undermine intelligence effectiveness by increasing the likelihood of micromanagement, as extrapolated in the fifth chapter. Certain aspects of the British intelligence community are already supervised proactively by the Commissioners. To build an additional layer of proactive oversight through the ISC, one that is unnecessary, would have negative repercussions on intelligence operations. Furthermore, another problem is that proactive supervision would likely weaken its position as an oversight body if it became known that it was complicit, even if ignorantly, in the running of a controversial operation without attempting to obstruct it. In particular, that complicity would essentially undermine the Committee's image as an independent body in relation to the agencies and the government. All indicating, of course, that the ISC's inability to oversee operations proactively is not a structural weakness, but a priority.

COMPLETE ACCESS TO INFORMATION

In the two previous sections on mandate and reporting, it was noted that complete access to information would allow the Committee to maximize the utility of the current structure without reforming the whole system. Although these may explain why complete access to information is necessary with regard to other aspects of the Committee, there is a further, more important reason for the necessity of complete access to information. Indeed, out of all the afore-mentioned criteria, none may be said to be as significant as access to information, for without information, an oversight body would merely wander in darkness and the public may question the credibility of what it has witnessed and reported. Faultless mandate, unlimited resources, independent reporting, or membership in a parliamentary oversight committee can never compensate for the lack of access to secret information. Indeed, the key characteristic that distinguishes the ISC from other parliamentary committees is, fundamentally, its access to classified information – personnel and documents. Currently, though the ISC may request information from the intelligence agencies, ministers have the authority to obstruct access to that information if it is deemed sensitive to national security. Before the Justice and Security Act 2013, on the other hand, the Committee could be blocked access to information by both ministers as well as heads of the three intelligence agencies. It is without doubt that the Justice and Security Act 2013 has somewhat improved the Committee's chances of gaining access to secret information. Despite that, however, it may still be argued that the reform did not go far enough because it did not give the Committee full access to information, a missing factor for attaining a truly effective oversight. Indeed, without complete information reports are incomplete and distorted;[117] by determining what part of the bigger picture reaches an audience, the executive and the agencies practically shape beliefs and perceptions, which precludes not only an 'objective' assessment (in a figurative sense) of intelligence activities, but also genuine transparency.

One way in which a case may be made against an oversight committee with full access to information is the argument that only on a few occasions has the ISC been actually obstructed from access to requested information, implying, in turn, that the power to access complete information is inevitably unnecessary. All in all, the problem with this view is that the real issue is not really the scarcity of information, but the lack of key information, without which the larger picture may not be completed.[118] This issue was illustrated by the Committee's investigations into the 2015 drone strikes in Syria. Above all, the major problem of the Committee in dealing with this issue was that the government refused to provide access to 'Ministerial submissions.' Through access to these submissions, the Committee was fundamentally hoping to gain insight into the factors that influenced ministerial decision-making process. It, rather, was given the classified documents upon which the 'Ministerial submissions' were based: the (unconvincing) reason being that there was no difference between the submissions and the classified documents. The government's decision to refuse access to this information was heavily criticized by the Committee. They stated that without access to that information, they could not determine the rationale behind the Foreign Minister's authorization. In a way, this did not allow the Committee to confirm their conclusions firmly. In the process, transparency was not sufficiently attained either. The Committee's inability to access full information, then, was a hindrance to its ability to undertake oversight effectively. A future reform of the Committee should take heed of this weakness above all else.

POLITICAL WILL

As our fifth criterion, political will is, alongside full access to information, the second most significant factor for effective parliamentary oversight. In particular, the Committee members need to have political will in the first place if they are to utilize their powers and authority. Without political will, even the most flawless oversight structures would be futile. This is best demonstrated by the difference in political will between the American and British oversight committees. It is no secret that the two American oversight committees (one in the Senate and the other in the House of Representatives) are renowned for their world-leading oversight structures: they have full access to classified information, are significantly independent, and possess great resources and staff. Yet, amidst such structural qualities, there are uncertainties about the maximum use of their potential. As Ken Robertson has illustrated, this has been witnessed on a number of occasions, most notably the Iran-Contra affair, when the committees' lack of interest in intelligence matters essentially allowed the agencies and the government to bypass their oversight. According to Loch K. Johnson's understanding of different types of oversight, the committees at the time exhibited the attitude of a 'police patrol' than that of a 'firefighter' on the alert.[119] The fact that Committee members change with each term may even foreshadow the impression that political will is unresolvable, unlike other structural weaknesses, because ultimately, it depends on each individual member and how they carry out their duties.

Notwithstanding that view, however, it would be mistaken to ignore the ways in which specific changes to an oversight committee's structure could facilitate political will. It is important, therefore, to understand the factors hindering strong political will. As Johnson has attested, the first significant obstacle that demotivates oversight members arises from the secrecy inherent in intelligence matters.[120] In particular, because they cannot inform the public about the exact things they do, they are effectively prevented from gaining public support for their efforts, taking into consideration the fact that public support is key for re-election. What is more, this issue is exacerbated by the usual public indifference to national security issues as opposed to, say, education or the health care system. To reduce the influence of these factors, Johnson recommends, for example, the use of perks and prizes for committee members who perform exceptionally well. Complementing these, he advises that the public should be properly informed on national security issues to improve their understanding of the role of committee members and how they are important. He suggests that a dialogue between academia and the people would prove useful in achieving this objective. The fact that there currently appears to be no explicit (nor implicit) references to such motivating mechanisms within the UK parliamentary oversight system indicates, indeed, the need for implementing such suggestions.

RECAPITULATION OF THE CHAPTER

To round off, in his *Meditations*, Marcus Aurelius held that change is a natural part of the universe, that it should not be feared but accepted; for there can be no warmth without wood burning and changing in form; nutrition without food digesting; nor any useful accomplishments, for that matter.[121] Change is not always popular; the unknown is feared; what is familiar is embraced. Nevertheless, change is inevitably necessary. Within the field of national security, this line of thinking was recently pursued by the Justice and Security Act 2013, which to some extent, changed the ISC. For the most part, these changes, however, were not profound but marginal, in that they did not threaten the core of what was already in place. Primarily, the act changed the Committee's membership, reporting, and mandate, but ignored the foremost aspect that required change, its need to have full access to information. As this chapter demonstrated, there are still clear weaknesses with the structure of the Committee. At the same time, however, it is understandable that the Justice and Security Act 2013 could not have addressed this without hindsight. Indeed, as was pointed out earlier, there is no ideal oversight framework in practice. Weaknesses are the starting point, and incremental improvements over the weaknesses are the ideal. In

any event, it does not seem likely that any meaningful change will be implemented any time soon. The
two-decade gap between the Committee's establishment and the Justice and Security Act 2013 seems to
foreshadow this suggestion. Notwithstanding, even
if the outcome may not lead to perfection, as it is
bound not to, inevitably it is clear that appropriate
change will need to be embraced in the near future
in all of the five aforementioned criteria if oversight
of the Intelligence and Security Committee is to become more effective.

CONCLUDING REMARKS
FOR PART II

The overarching incentive behind this research, principally, has been to push forward academic debates and policies on the parliamentary committee oversight of the British intelligence community. In fulfilling that objective, three sub-themes have been addressed in turn. The first, essentially, aimed to justify the motive for intelligence oversight through an assessment of this oversight's impact on intelligence effectiveness and accountability. In short, it was argued that criticisms of oversight (respectively, the futility of external oversight, leaks, and micromanagement) are generally unfounded and that, contrastingly, there is overwhelming evidence in favor of better oversight: both on a conceptual level (in terms of enhancing democratic accountability) and a practical level (enhancing intelligence effectiveness). With that justification in mind, the second sub-theme then continued the overarching aim of better intelligence oversight in the United Kingdom by offering a preliminary performance assessment of the Intelligence and Security Committee (ISC) to determine the current state of a significant oversight mechanism within the country. It was maintained that the ISC's most recent activities exhibited a mixed picture based on two criteria: influence on policies and agencies' activities, and contributions to transparency. In continuation of that narrative, the third sub-theme accordingly sought a greater understanding of better oversight by assessing the ISC's structural qualities: in essence, the underlying causes that determine performance. After assessing five criteria (membership, reporting, mandate, access to information and political will), it concluded that this body, even though requiring some degree of reform, should be given full access to information as the most urgent advance.

On the whole, it should be mentioned here that this research undertaking contributes to both current academic literature, as well as possible policymaking. Respecting the former, it helped to fill a gap in the literature regarding the ISC's performance in its pursuits (from March 2015 until September 2017) and its structural strengths and weaknesses (after the Justice and Security Act 2013 reform). In this sense, it has offered a contemporary picture of the ISC. Additionally, in addressing the second sub-theme of the essay, it identified (for the first time) methodological problems regarding the theoretical framework of the topic, as well as two criteria that could assuredly be used for a future assessment of the Intelligence and Security Committee's accomplishments. Coupled with those items, the contribution to policymaking essentially proceeded from those areas outlining specific needs to be reformed if oversight is to function constructively in the future, including complete access to information, increasing political will, or clearer reports better aimed at raising public education.

Those issues being stated, it is important to note that there is still significant room for further research in this field. In particular, the research could be considerably extended by incorporating comparisons with parliamentary oversight committees of other democratic states (such as the United States, Canada, Australia, and European states) in assessing performance, along with structural properties, and accordingly recommend alternate possibilities – hence procuring best practices. Indeed, an additional area to investigate would be in assessing the significance of Britain's ISC in comparison to other oversight mechanisms, particularly the Commissioners and the Tribunal, of course bearing in mind the reforms to the oversight system in the aftermath of the Justice and Security Act 2013 and most importantly the Investigatory Powers Act 2016 (for example, the introduction of a single Commissioner to replace the previous three Commissioners). A third option, alternatively, would be to seek a theoretically ideal framework for assessing the performance and structure of intelligence oversight. The absence of such a theory currently poses a significant methodological hurdle for more comprehensive research in the area of intelligence oversight. Combined with a comparison to the oversight systems of other states, individual oversight mechanisms within a state, not to mention institutions similar to oversight bodies within the same state (parliamentary select committees, especially), may allow gradual steps to be undertaken towards a better oversight system.

Finally, in bringing this discussion to a close, it is important to remind ourselves, yet again, of the uncertainty that lies ahead. In particular, the security environment is a constantly changing phenomenon, one that inherently shapes national security policies and, more importantly, citizens' perceptions of their safety and security. Fear is the essential ingredient in this process. Depending on perceptions of national security and the security environment, it can either rise or fall, resulting consequently in differing priorities and responses that change accordingly: while the former may increase public demand for expanding security (by relaxing restrictions on the intelligence agencies), the latter would likely prioritize liberty (thus, expecting greater restrictions on intelligence practices). What is, above all, important in this discussion is that the larger picture, and especially the long-term perspective, should not be neglected in exchange for the more tempting short-term perspective. The danger, otherwise, would – as it was attested to in the first chapter – not only be intelligence ineffectiveness but, more importantly, democratic unaccountability. The fact that intelligence oversight in the UK is still debated and maintained – evident in the passing of the Justice and Security Act 2013 and Investigatory Powers Act 2016 – is, doubtless, commendable. Nonetheless, as demonstrated in the final two chapters, there is still significant room for improvement. It is in taking this view into account that this research paper should conclude with the statement that further progress in the work and structure of the Intelligence and Security Committee should be pursued with conviction.

APPENDIX

CLASSICAL AND SOCIAL LIBERALS ON THE
APPROPRIATE RANGE OF STATE ACTIVITIES

The proper business of governments, or the full extent of their activities, is liable to some controversy in politics. There is nothing in such topics which is not the subject of debate and in which liberals of learning, whether they be classical or social, are not of contrary opinions. We shall briefly examine each of these in order, beginning with classical liberals, and shall weigh some considerations concerning the most proper general and particular activities of the state. According to Classical Liberalism, which is so obvious and natural, in general, state activities must be reduced to a minimum and be incapable of any further diminution. In this respect, I am reminded of some authors, from John Locke and Monsieur Tocqueville, to Adam Smith and Thomas Malthus, etc. On the other hand, Social Liberalism,[122] which succeeded Classical Liberalism, arose gradually in the nineteenth century, when poverty, poor working conditions, ignorance, and other objects of this kind, which contain something adverse, pleaded in favor of an enlargement of the sphere of state activity; which perhaps in its turn is favorable to the doctrine of the welfare state. It is sufficient to observe on this occasion that the welfare state may be defined to be 'an interventionist state which goes beyond the minimal state functions of providing [defense] and security of property, and legislates to improve people's well-being (through a provision of welfare social security [programs] like free education, health care, and so forth).'

WHY MINIMAL GOVERNMENT IS NECESSARY

Upon examination, there are a number of reasons commonly produced for the Classical Liberal opinion to be satisfactory. The first principle is that 'individuals should enjoy the widest possible liberty.' Hence, as a notable classical liberal, John Locke asserted, that 'since man is a free being who knows his own interests best, an authoritarian or paternalistic government is against human nature.' Additionally, J. S. Mill stated that a government may not intervene, notwithstanding all their abstractions and refinements, in the power of any person to harm themselves, or 'to bring an individual into conformity with the received moral ideas of his community.' Therefore, they argue that the role of the state should be, when considered, proportioned to the creation of 'a framework of peace and social order within which private citizens can conduct their lives as they think best.' This end, needless to say, is agreeable to 'modern' classical liberals (i.e., libertarians), such as Robert Nozick, who famously said, that the 'night-watchman state' of Classical Liberalism should be 'limited to the functions of protecting all its citizens against violence, theft, and fraud, and the enforcement of contracts and so on.' In which instance, I affirm there are three main functions of the state conveyed by the defenders of this hypothesis. The first is the execution of law and order, and they attain it by 'some kind of machinery,' such as law enforcement agencies, viz. the police. The creation of a court of judicature is esteemed as a second species of the state functions, to better assure people of the moral obligation, validity, and concurrence of all contracts or voluntary agreements betwixt the parties. Finally, the state is also responsible for the creation of armed forces to protect the public from foreign threats. So, on the whole, Classical Liberalism concludes that society proceeds from these original principles, without the intervention of economic and social assistance, a question which must necessarily 'be left entirely in the hands of individuals or private businesses.' Thus it more easily attains that economic situation when it is of a competitive, efficient, and productive nature, and contains some things prosperous for individuals who are at liberty 'to rise and fall according to their talents and willingness to work.'

OF THE ORIGIN OF SOCIAL LIBERALISM

However useful, or even necessary, the stability of absolute individual freedom may be to Classical Liberalism, it is attended with very considerable inconveniences. To apply a remedy directly, Social Liberalism expresses a resolution of establishing a system of welfare social security 'designed to reduce poverty and social inequality' by attempting 'a wholesale redistribution of wealth through a comprehensive system of public services and state benefits, financed through progressive taxation.' And of this nature, Social Liberalism is understood to be in most European states. For instance, social liberals in the United Kingdom exert the productive quality of Keynesian economics, by which John Maynard Keynes was determined to 'reduce unemployment and promote growth.' It is evident, then, that Social Liberalism is an eager exponent of nationalization and the mixed economy: While so far as their succor extended, so far have social liberals, like Hobhouse and Green, promoted that 'the doctrine of liberty should not prevent the general will from acting, where it must, for the common good.' I must further add, that as an object of their reasoning, the 1942 Beveridge Report became an example to others as the model or archetype, from which social liberals derived the protection of ordinary individuals from the ' "five giants" of want, disease, ignorance, squalor, and idleness, and to extend this protection "from the cradle to the grave." ' Here then, is a kind of inference which Social Liberalism employs in enabling citizens to choose the means, and choose also the end of their lives; since self is supposed to flow from that solidity and force which attend their individual potential that is established by the convention 'to help individuals to help themselves.'

LIMITATIONS OF CLASSICAL LIBERALISM

If we carry our inquiry beyond the appearances of Classical Liberalism, one finds good reasons for skepticism. To begin with the first criticism; Social Liberalism argues that the market system of *laissez-faire* capitalism does not and cannot, even if it is perfectly constant, grant whatever the public demands (viz. common goods like roads and hospitals) due to its contradictions and imperfections. Considered as such, the state must in some respects 'help those whom the market system neglects because their demands are not backed by cash;' so that Mançur Olson and Kenneth Arrow approve of that expeditious way; that though individuals will be inclined contrary to that opinion of the necessity of their contribution to the provision of public goods, the choice falls on their particular governments to intervene in order 'to make everyone contribute fairly to the cost of public or collective goods,' even if those individuals show a reserve and doubt in doing others justice.

Furthermore, although Social Liberalism may, in appearance, be incompatible with Classical Liberalism, yet it can always be made evident that the former species of Liberalism still 'operates in the spirit of the liberal model,' and that by providing a 'minimum subsistence to the worst-off members of society,' they quickly enhance their equality of opportunity; as by an observance of the rules of justice, they can preserve fair competition, and keep themselves from falling into that unstable and unpredictable condition, which is commonly represented as the state of capitalism.

It has been observed, in treating the principle of self-ownership, 'that everyone has the right to the fruits of their labor and to anything received in free exchange.' But, what strikes egalitarians with vivacity, agrees with the idea of enjoying all the fruits of labor, since they are derived from their very collective nature and essence of society, which arises from 'a framework of shared institutions, laws, and structures.' But society also has a secondary function, as John Rawls will tell us, and this function is nothing but 'a cooperative project for mutual advantage,' which proceeds from the notion that because 'social and economic advantages (such as family status and education) are unearned and undeserved.' From this, it follows, that their talents and skills are undeserved and unearned (i.e., it is due to some lucky circumstance).

OF SKEPTICISM WITH REGARD TO SOCIAL LIBERALISM

I shall now proceed to the examination of the speculative and practical reasonings for skepticism concerning Social Liberalism. In the former case, the New Right ideologues often expect, from all common welfare and social security systems, that they will neglect 'individualism and personal responsibility,' and be irresponsible by their unacceptable levels of taxation. Accordingly, they may observe that this creates the 'culture of dependency' when its poor are enslaved (so to speak) by their dependence on government aid. Nay, Charles Murray and George Gilder go further and assert that job creation schemes not only 'pushed up unemployment by weakening individual initiative,' it also convinced the same persons who were placed under the terms of 'unemployed,' 'handicapped' or 'disadvantaged,' were often the 'victims of circumstances.' For this reason, it is more necessary, Murray believes, for them to separate social security from the central government, whereas they ought to allow some local communities and societies, in which individual or communal incentives at least might be encouraged.

So stated, I shall add the consideration of another criticism that is ascribed to Social Liberalism. Some socialists fix their attention on the arguments proving the probability of its deepening social inequalities instead of reducing them. Julian Le Grand, therefore, maintains a very extravagant paradox. This paradox is that the prosperous and the educated chiefly, instead of the less prosperous and the uneducated, take advantage of the services provided by the state (e.g., health care, rail services), as they are more likely better informed and aware of these privileges. Additionally, Marxists extend this analysis beyond its original bounds; since it is certain that, in their thinking, social security serves to conceal the original facts and realities of class tyranny and oppression, by means of the force of government aid, which cuts off all hope of ever attaining class consciousness, instead of the sentiments of proletariat morals, which always attends revolutions. Not to mention that it is only from the provision social welfare makes for 'the productive needs of the economic system,' that capitalism exploits the educated and healthy workforce for its designed ends. The last critique I shall take notice of is, that according to the general notions of Malthus and Herbert Spencer, the poor are poor because they are 'undeserving' of government aid, because the idea of the 'survival of the fittest' requires that every inferior strain be eliminated in order to tend to the promotion of 'the eventual physical and moral perfection of the race.' Either way, the absurdity of both extremes is a demonstration of the susceptibility of this medium.

CONCLUSION OF THIS APPENDIX

In general, the following reflections seem satisfactory. Some observers borrow from preceding experience, viz. that it is usual for a *laissez-faire* economy to operate for the public good, being seconded by the extensive privatization of these industries. This phenomenon was first established on the testimony of Thatcher's Neoliberal policies, by a visible gradation, which led some people backward in their footsteps to ask, 'Why shouldn't private enterprise provide this service, rather than the state?' Nor does this sentiment rest there. Nozick believes we are entitled to what we get out of our talents and skills, since they must be part of our character, whereas it is difficult to admit division into natural talents and hard work. So private property, however justifiable the opposition may be by the general rules of Social Liberalism, is inseparable from the individual.

To talk instead of objections and balancing of arguments Malthus and Spencer employ in their inquiries is to confess, either that each person has a right to a decent life, as it is stated in the 'liberal declarations of human rights,' or that Spencer's moral argument, arising from analogy, might be mistaken in asserting, that 'evolution does not operate in society,' and that the existence of 'the less adequate members of society does not weaken the structure or health of the "social whole." ' Anti-paternalistic opinions may be difficult to be repudiated, because of the uneasiness, that particular examples cause to their effect. Meanwhile, I shall observe one example, still belonging to this subject. Suppose that a welfare state imitates William Burroughs' 'Freeland' (a fictional state in *The Naked Lunch*), wherein every person can indulge in every thing, provided for by the state; here, it is evident that the 'independence of the individual and her free, rational status' would needs be surrendered to the state. Yet being more universal and constant, some counterbalance the latter in interpretation, and admit of the doubt, that 'intervention is not made paternalistically, but, rather, in the interests of maintaining the precondition of liberal society.'

I am certain that the strengths and weaknesses in both these ways of considering Liberalism are conspicuous. However, from the consideration of the association of ideas above-explained, it appears that, on the whole, we can seek in Classical Liberalism a stronger and more convincing argument, which appears very probable in practice, because the opposite philosophy of Social Liberalism encourages prodigality, irresponsibility, irresolution and disincentivizes its recipient for business and action. Or the contrary, the doctrine of Social Liberalism may generally be better received in theory than its antagonist, because it is interested in the moral quality of the person, as to be sensible of their good and fortune. This evidence in the deductions may seduce us unwarily into the opinion that state functions should grow out of regard to its moral obligation, yet never by carrying too far it ceases to induce responsibility amongst human creatures.

Anyway, to convince us more fully of this conclusion, I shall take a general review of the preceding reasonings of the two kinds of Liberalism. Classical Liberalism values the minimal state upon the supposition, that it amounts to freedom in the highest degree of such as are possible in their frame and constitution of law and justice, which is advantageous to the security and protection of the individual's freedom and property. Social Liberalism, on the other hand, appreciates the importance of the state's duty to provide welfare services, even though there be a real necessity that they impose a tax (enlarged above the share required by Classical Liberalism) upon their subjects: for which reason, Social Liberalism accuses Classical Liberalism of the neglect of each person's right to a modest and decent life as the standard of equality or inequality. Accordingly, we find that by benefits and drawbacks, both traditions produce difficult obstacles to surmount or elude, and which we desire to balance on any side, however cold and unentertaining, once brought in as subservient to practical morality, and may render this latter aim more persuasive in its exhortations.

AUTHOR'S AFTERWORD

It has been my design to enter into the deepest and dirtiest pits of corruption which have reduced so many millions to a merciless subservience. Yet, there was a time when I first considered with the most reverential awe the mysteries of *arcana imperii* or state-freemasonry; but philosophy, experience and age have rent the veil of the establishment of these errand boys; and I confess I view this den, without any reserve, with the utmost abhorrence. But here, let me give a glance at the whole history of our proceedings.

I wrote these essays during the course of my academic readings at Aberystwyth University for a bachelor's degree in International Politics and Intelligence Studies, and a master's in Intelligence and Strategic Studies. One of the earliest attempts in the technical understanding of this field of intelligence was prepared by this educational corporation. And indeed, Aberystwyth was the university where Intelligence Studies was formally studied and taught before a succession of similar programs of study in that part of the world emerged to light. Personally, my involvements in these arts, or the lack thereof, I will not affirm. In this case, therefore, I will let them repose in my own bosom. Yet, allowing all this, it will be found that the arguments and ideas upon which these papers are founded were derived from the perusal of those prejudicial misrepresentations – by a young man who at the same time had impressed on his imagination the pictures of James Bond, Ethan Hunt in the *Mission: Impossible* films, and Jason Bourne; or some other shadowy being without substance or effect, such as Sam Fisher in Tom Clancy's *Splinter Cell* or Altaïr Ibn-La'Ahad in the *Assassin's Creed* video game franchise. Indeed, if I wrote merely to please the palate of my examiners, my mind was soon made to grow unwilling, enervate and utterly incapable of knowing the true nature of a business: at once so disagreeable and odious. I admit they are forever toads or cankerworms: *medio de fonte leporum surgit aliquid amari quod in ipsis floribus angat.*[123] This is nothing else than a strong confirmation of David William Parry's notions of the ruling elite, whose hearts are torn by avarice, by the horrid effects of fraud, by destructive open injustice and every sort of personal gratification. In all appearance, power has extirpated from their minds the remains of their virtue.

For my part, as an historian, philosopher, and educator, I am pretty well convinced that the whole principle of our education is totally corrupted, whether it is or is not dependent on the state. And indeed, schools and universities seem to be the indoctrination centers where the pretended wise revelations of social science, which (we may be sure) must establish such a fund of rewards as will make the amplest allowance for every possible research, have done very near as much mischief as they can do, to our relish for global peace, public morality, and uninterrupted prosperity. Because too great a superficial discourse concerning the relations that surround us weakens the solidity and depth of philosophical inquiry. The reader sees that I can assign no reason why spycraft, or surveillance, should be paid for by oppressive taxes. And, after all, what do we gain by "national security," but a source of imaginary terrors that must, therefore, manufacture the consent of the people?

I have purposely not avoided a parade of eloquence for the most part, because I despise the slaughter of the human mind, and, on comparing it with imitative technologies, do not admit that every species of artificial intelligence is good. The ChatGPT chatbot! The ChatGPT chatbot is the last act of my life that I shall utilize! Either way, during the course of my discussion you may have observed a very striking distinction in the style and tenor between the two parts. This is because the materials in the second part relate to the pursuits of my present studies for a doctoral degree. In these early and unrefined judgments, I have not entered very minutely into every particular that regards intelligence oversight; whereas I thought it better to limit its signification until I can secure the most satisfactory analysis in my next book.

In the meantime, I hope readers of this present volume will find some worth and value within these texts.

BIBLIOGRAPHY

BOOKS

Allhoff, Fritz. 'An Ethical Defense of Torture in Interrogation.' In *Ethics of Spying: A Reader for the Intelligence Professional*, edited by Jan Goldman, 126-140. Oxford: Scarecrow Press, 2006.

Andrew, Christopher, and David Dilks. Introduction to *The Missing Dimension: Governments and Intelligence Communities in the Twentieth Century*, edited by Christopher Andrew and David Dilks, 1-16. London: Palgrave Macmillan, 1984.

Andrew, Christopher. *The Defence of the Realm: The Authorized History of MI5*. London: Penguin Books, 2010.

Andrew, Christopher. *The Secret World: A History of Intelligence*. London: Penguin, 2019.

Baldino, Daniel. 'Introduction: Watching the Watchmen.' In *Democratic Oversight of Intelligence Services*, edited by Daniel Baldino, 1-32. Annandale, NSW: The Federation Press, 2010.

Bar-Joseph, Uri, and Rose McDermott. 'The Intelligence Analysis Crisis.' In *The Oxford Handbook of National Security Intelligence*, edited by Loch K. Johnson, 359-374. Oxford: Oxford University Press, 2010.

Bochel, Hugh, and Andrew Defty. 'Parliamentary Oversight of Intelligence Agencies: Lessons from Westminster.' In *Security in a Small Nation: Scotland, Democracy, Politics*, edited by Andrew W. Neal, 103-124. Cambridge, UK: Open Book Publishers, 2017. https://www.jstor.org/stable/j.ctt1sq5v42.9.

Caparini, Marina. 'Controlling and Overseeing Intelligence Services in Democratic States.' In *Democratic Control of Intelligence Services: Containing Rogue Elephants*, edited by Hans Born and Marina Caparini, 3-24. London: Routledge, 2007.

Caravelli, Jack. 'Lessons from the Iranian case and the changing face of American intelligence.' In *Intelligence and Human Rights in the Era of Global Terrorism*, edited by Steve Tsang, 26-38. Westport, CT; London: Praeger Security International, 2007.

Clarke, Richard A., and Robert K. Knake. *Cyber War: The Next Threat to National Security and What to Do About It*. New York: HarperCollins Publishers, 2010.

Coleman, E. Gabriella. *Coding Freedom: The Ethics and Aesthetics of Hacking*. Princeton; Oxford: Princeton University Press, 2013. https://doi.org/10.2307/j.ctt1r2gbj.

Curran, James, Natalie Fenton, and Des Freedman. *Misunderstanding the Internet*. London: Routledge, 2012.

Davies, Philip H. J. 'Britain's machinery of intelligence accountability: realistic oversight in the absence of moral panic.' In *Democratic Oversight of Intelligence Services*, edited by Daniel Baldino, 133-160. Annandale, NSW: The Federation Press, 2010.

Dulles, Allen W. *The Craft of Intelligence: America's Legendary Spy Master on the Fundamentals of Intelligence Gathering for a Free World*. Guilford, CT: The Lyons Press, 2006.

Elias, Norbert. *The Civilizing Process: Sociogenetic and Psychogenetic Investigations*. Edited by Eric Dunning, Johan

Goudsblom and Stephen Mennell. Translated by Edmund Jephcott. Rev. ed. Oxford: Blackwell Publishers, 2000.

Gill, Peter, and Mark Phythian. *Intelligence in an Insecure World* 2nd ed. Cambridge: Polity, 2012.

Gill, Peter. "'A Formidable Power to Cause Trouble for the Government"? Intelligence Oversight and the Creation of the UK Intelligence and Security Committee.' In *Learning from the Secret Past: Cases in British Intelligence History*, edited by Robert Dover and Michael S. Goodman, 43-63. Washington, DC: Georgetown University Press, 2011.

Gill, Peter. *Policing Politics: Security Intelligence and the Liberal Democratic State*. London: Frank Cass, 1994.

Godfrey, J. E. Drexel. 'Ethics and Intelligence.' In *Ethics of Spying: A Reader for the Intelligence Professional*, edited by Jan Goldman, 1-17. Lanham, MD: Scarecrow Press, 2006.

Goodwin, Barbara. *Using Political Ideas*. 4th ed. Chichester: John Wiley & Sons, 1997.

Gray, John. *Liberalisms: Essays in Political Philosophy*. London: Routledge, 1989.

Hastedt, Glenn P. 'Controlling Intelligence: Defining the Problem.' In *Controlling Intelligence*, edited by Glenn P. Hastedt, 3-22. London: Frank Cass, 1991.

Haswell, Jock. *Spies and Spymasters: A Concise History of Intelligence*. London: Thames and Hudson, 1977.

Heywood, Andrew. *Political Ideas and Concepts: An Introduction*. London: Palgrave Macmillan, 1994.

Hillebrand, Claudia. 'Intelligence Oversight and Accountability.' In *Routledge Companion to Intelligence Studies*, edited by Robert Dover, Michael S. Goodman and Claudia Hillebrand, 305-312. London: Routledge, 2013.

Hulnick, Arthur S., and David W. Mattausch. 'Ethics and Morality in U.S. Secret Intelligence.' In *Ethics of Spying: A Reader for the Intelligence Professional*, edited by Jan Goldman, 39-51. Lanham, MD: Scarecrow Press, 2006.

Jeffreys-Jones, Rhodri. Preface to *Intelligence Studies in Britain and the US: Historiography Since 1945*, edited by Christopher R. Moran and Christopher J. Murphy, xv-xviii. Edinburgh: Edinburgh University Press, 2013.

Jeffreys-Jones, Rhodri. 'The Rise and Fall of the CIA.' In *The Oxford Handbook of National Security Intelligence*, edited by Loch K. Johnson, 122-137. Oxford: Oxford University Press, 2010.

Johnson, Loch K. 'Intelligence Oversight in the United States.' In *Intelligence and Human Rights in the Era of Global Terrorism*, edited by Steve Tsang, 54-66. Westport, CT; London: Praeger Security International, 2007.

Jones, R. V. *Reflections on Intelligence*. London: Heinemann, 1989.

Jones, R. V. *Reflections on Intelligence*. London: Mandarin, 1990.

Knightley, Phillip. *The Second Oldest Profession: Spies and Spying in the Twentieth Century*. New York; London: W. W. Norton & Company, 1987.

Kukathas, Chandran, and Philip Pettit. *Rawls: A Theory of Justice and its Critics*. Cambridge; Malden, MA: Polity Press, 1990.

Linklater, Andrew. 'Process sociology and international

relations.' In *Norbert Elias and Figurational Research: Processual Thinking in Sociology*, edited by Norman Gabriel and Stephen Mennell, 48-64. Malden, MA: Wiley-Blackwell/Sociological Review, 2011.

Linklater, Andrew. *The Problem of Harm in World Politics: Theoretical Investigations*. Cambridge: Cambridge University Press, 2011.

Lowenthal, Mark M. *Intelligence: From Secrets to Policy*. 7th ed. Los Angeles: CQ Press, 2016.

Morrison, John N. L. 'Political Supervision of Intelligence Services in the United Kingdom.' In *Intelligence and Human Rights in the Era of Global Terrorism*, edited by Steve Tsang, 41-53. Westport, CT; London: Praeger Security International, 2007.

Pekel, Kent. 'The Need for Improvement: Integrity, Ethics, and the CIA.' In *Ethics of Spying: A Reader for the Intelligence Professional*, edited by Jan Goldman, 52-65. Lanham, MD: Scarecrow Press, 2006.

Richards, Julian. *The Art and Science of Intelligence Analysis*. Oxford: Oxford University Press, 2010.

Russell, Richard L. 'Competitive Analysis: Techniques for Better Gauging Enemy Political Intentions and Military Capabilities.' In *The Oxford Handbook of National Security Intelligence*, edited by Loch K. Johnson, 375-388. Oxford: Oxford University Press, 2010.

Scott, Len, and Peter Jackson. 'Journeys in Shadows: Introduction.' In *Understanding Intelligence in the Twenty-First Century: Journeys in Shadows*, edited by Len Scott and Peter Jackson, 1-28. London; New York: Routledge, 2004.

Shulsky, Abram N., and Gary J. Schmitt. *Silent Warfare: Understanding the World of Intelligence*. 3rd ed. Washington:

Potomac Books, 2002.

Smits, Katherine. *Applying Political Theory: Issues and Debates*. London: Palgrave Macmillan, 2009.

Treverton, Gregory F. 'Addressing "Complexities" in Homeland Security.' In *The Oxford Handbook of National Security Intelligence*, edited by Loch K. Johnson, 343-358. Oxford: Oxford University Press, 2010.

Tsang, Steve. 'Stopping Global Terrorism and Protecting Rights.' In *Intelligence and Human Rights in the Era of Global Terrorism*, edited by Steve Tsang, 1-14. Westport, CT; London: Praeger Security International, 2007.

Whitaker, Reg. *The End of Privacy: How Total Surveillance Is Becoming a Reality*. New York: The New Press, 1999.

Whittaker, Jason. *The Cyberspace Handbook*. London; New York: Routledge, 2003.

Wight, Martin. *Systems of States*. Edited by Hedley Bull. Leicester: Leicester University Press, 1977.

Wilson, Peter. 'Preparing to Meet New Challenges.' In *Intelligence and Human Rights in the Era of Global Terrorism*, edited by Steve Tsang, 111-120. Westport, CT; London: Praeger Security International, 2007.

Wright, Peter, and Paul Greengrass. *Spycatcher: The Candid Autobiography of a Senior Intelligence Officer*. London: Viking, 1987.

Zegart, Amy B. *Eyes on Spies: Congress and the United States Intelligence Community*. Stanford, CA: Hoover Institution Press, 2011.

JOURNAL ARTICLES

Aldrich, Richard J. 'Beyond the Vigilant State: Globalisation and Intelligence.' *Review of International Studies* 35, no. 4 (2009): 889-902. http://www.jstor.org/stable/40588091.

Aldrich, Richard J. 'Global Intelligence Co-operation versus Accountability: New Facets to an Old Problem.' *Intelligence and National Security* 24, no. 1 (2009): 26-56. https://doi.org/10.1080/02684520902756812.

Barry, Christian. 'A Challenge to the Reigning Theory of the Just War.' *International Affairs* 87, no. 2 (2011): 457-466. https://www.jstor.org/stable/20869670.

Bellaby, Ross. 'What's The Harm? The Ethics of Intelligence Collection.' *Intelligence and National Security* 27, no. 1 (2012): 93-117. https://doi.org/10.1080/02684527.2012.621600.

Bellamy, Alex J. 'Dirty Hands and Lesser Evils in the War on Terror.' *The British Journal of Politics and International Relations* 9, no. 3 (2007): 509-526. https://doi.org/10.1111/j.1467-856x.2006.00255.x.

Bufacchi, Vittorio, and Jean Maria Arrigo. 'Torture, Terrorism and the State: A Refutation of the Ticking-Bomb Argument.' *Journal of Applied Philosophy* 23, no. 3 (2006): 355-373. https://www.jstor.org/stable/24355182.

Carroll, Thomas Patrick. 'The Case Against Intelligence Openness.' *International Journal of Intelligence and CounterIntelligence* 14, no. 4 (2001): 559-574.

Collet, Tanja. 'Civilization and civilized in post-9/11 US presidential speeches.' *Discourse & Society* 20, no. 4 (2009): 455-475 https://www.jstor.org/stable/42889273.

Dinstein, Yoram. 'The Principle of Distinction and Cyber War in International Armed Conflicts.' *Journal of Conflict and Security Law* 17, no. 2 (Summer 2012): 261-277. https://doi.org/10.1093/jcsl/krs015.

Dipert, Randall R. 'The Ethics of Cyberwarfare.' *Journal of Military Ethics* 9, no. 4 (2010): 384-410. https://doi.org/10.1080/15027570.2010.536404.

Erskine, Toni. "As Rays of Light to the Human Soul?' Moral Agents and Intelligence Gathering.' *Intelligence and National Security* 19, no. 2 (2004): 359-381. https://doi.org/10.1080/02684520420003 02047.

Gill, Peter. 'Evaluating intelligence oversight committees: The UK Intelligence and Security Committee and the 'war on terror." *Intelligence and National Security* 22, no. 1 (2007): 14-37. https://doi.org/10.1080/02684520701200756.

Gill, Peter. 'Intelligence, Threat, Risk and the Challenge of Oversight.' *Intelligence and National Security* 27, no. 2 (2012): 206-222. https://doi.org/10.1080/02684527.2012.661643.

Herman, Michael. 'Ethics and Intelligence after September 2001.' *Intelligence and National Security* 19, no. 2 (2004): 342-358. https://doi.org/10.1080/0268452042000302038.

Honig, Or Arthur, and Sarah Zimskind. 'The Spy Machine and the Ballot Box: Examining Democracy's Intelligence Advantage.' *International Journal of Intelligence and CounterIntelligence* 30, no. 3 (2017): 431-463. https://doi.org/10.1080/08850607.2017.1263 524.

Kahn, David. 'An Historical Theory of Intelligence.' *Intelligence and National Security* 16, no. 3 (2001): 79-92. https://doi.org/10.10 80/02684520412331306220.

Krieken, Robert van. 'The barbarism of civilization: cultural genocide and the 'stolen generations." *British Journal of Sociology* 50, no. 2 (June 1999): 297-315. https://onlinelibrary.wiley.com/ doi/abs/10.1111/j.1468-4446.1999.00297.x.

Linklater, Andrew, and Stephen Mennell. 'Norbert Elias, The Civilizing Process: Sociogenetic And Psychogenetic Investigations—An Overview And Assessment.' *History and Theory* 49, no. 3 (October 2010): 384-411. https://www.jstor.org/ stable/40864499.

Linklater, Andrew. 'International Society and the Civilizing Process.' *Ritsumeikan International Affairs* 9 (2011): 1-26.

Linklater, Andrew. 'Torture and Civilisation.' *International Relations* 21, no. 1 (2007): 111-118. https://doi. org/10.1177/0047117807073771.

Marion, Nancy E. 'The Council of Europe's Cyber Crime Treaty: An exercise in Symbolic Legislation.' *International Journal of Cyber Criminology* 4, no. 1/2 (Jan-Dec 2010): 699-712. https:// www.cybercrimejournal.com/pdf/marion2010ijcc.pdf.

Newbery, Samantha. 'Terrorism, Torture and Intelligence.' *International Politics* 50, no. 4 (2013): 512-531. DOI:10.1057/ip.2013.20

Omand, Sir David, and Mark Phythian. 'Ethics and Intelligence: A Debate.' *International Journal of Intelligence and Counterintelligence* 26, no. 1 (2013): 38-63. DOI: 10.1080/08850607.2012.705186.

Omand, Sir David. 'Can we have the Pleasure of the Grin without Seeing the Cat? Must the Effectiveness of Secret Agencies Inevitably Fade on Exposure to the Light?' *Intelligence and National Security* 23, no. 5 (2008): 593-607. https://doi. org/10.1080/02684520802449476.

Pfaff, Tony, and Jeffrey R. Tiel. 'The Ethics of Espionage.' *Journal of Military Ethics* 3, no. 1 (2004): 1-15. https://doi.org/10.1080/15027570310004447.

Quinlan, Michael. 'Just Intelligence: Prolegomena to an Ethical Theory.' *Intelligence and National Security* 22, no. 1 (2007): 1-13. https://doi.org/10.1080/02684520701200715.

Rid, Thomas. 'Cyber War Will Not Take Place.' *Journal of Strategic Studies* 35, no. 1 (2012): 5-32. https://doi.org/10.1080/01402390.2011.608939.

Roberts, Alasdair. 'WikiLeaks: the illusion of transparency.' *International Review of Administrative Sciences* 78, no. 1 (2012): 116-133. https://doi.org/10.1177/0020852311429428.

Rudner, Martin. 'Hunters and Gatherers: The Intelligence Coalition Against Islamic Terrorism.' *International Journal of Intelligence and CounterIntelligence* 17, no. 2 (2004): 193-230. https://doi.org/10.1080/08850600490274890.

Spence, Richard B. 'Secret Agent 666: Aleister Crowley and British Intelligence in America, 1914-1918.' *International Journal of Intelligence and CounterIntelligence* 13, no. 3 (2000): 359-371. https://doi.org/10.1080/08850600050140634.

Stoddart, Kristan. 'Live Free or Die Hard: U.S.-UK Cybersecurity Policies.' *Political Science Quarterly* 131, no. 4 (Winter 2016): 803-842. https://doi.org/10.1002/polq.12535.

Sussman, David. 'What's Wrong with Torture?' *Philosophy & Public Affairs* 33, no. 1 (2005): 1-33. https://doi.org/10.1111/j.1088-4963.2005.00023.x.

WEBSITES

BBC. 'UK spy watchdog "taken in" by security agencies - MP.' February 27, 2015. https://www.bbc.co.uk/news/election-2015-31665312.

Borger, Julian, Patrick Wintour, and Jessica Elgot. 'Trump stands by unsubstantiated claim that British intelligence spied on him.' *The Guardian*, March 17, 2017. https://www.theguardian.com/us-news/2017/mar/17/white-house-will-not-be-repeat-claims-gchq-spied-trump-.

Branigan, Tania. 'Rifkind says he'll stand against Davis.' *The Guardian*, June 8, 2005. https://www.theguardian.com/politics/2005/jun/08/uk.toryleadership2005.

Britannica, The Editors of Encyclopaedia. 'Categorical Imperative.' *Encyclopedia Britannica.* February 10, 2023. https://www.britannica.com/topic/categorical-imperative.

Clarke, Richard A. 'Cyberwar in 2013.' Filmed December 8, 2012 in New York City. The Economist's World in 2013 Festival, 21:27. https://www.youtube.com/watch?v=6_ek8mugOUc.

Defty, Andrew. 'General Election 2017: The Unwelcome Impact on the Work of the Intelligence and Security Committee.' *RUSI Commentary* (blog). RUSI. May 10, 2017. https://rusi.org/explore-our-research/publications/commentary/general-election-2017-unwelcome-impact-work-intelligence-and-security-committee.

Defty, Andrew. 'Recent events at the Intelligence and Security Committee make it increasingly difficult to justify the current arrangements for scrutinising the security services.' *Democratic Audit UK* (blog). May 30, 2014. https://www.democraticaudit.com/2014/05/30/recent-events-at-the-intelligence-and-security-committee-make-it-increasingly-difficult-to-justify-the-current-arrangements-for-scrutinising-the-security-services/.

Dennis, M. Aaron. 'Cybercrime.' *Encyclopedia Britannica*. December 15, 2022. https://www.britannica.com/topic/cybercrime.

Driver, Julia, 'The History of Utilitarianism.' In *The Stanford Encyclopedia of Philosophy*, edited by Edward N. Zalta and Uri Nodelman. Winter 2022 ed. https://plato.stanford.edu/archives/win2022/entries/utilitarianism-history/.

Foster, Alice. 'Terror attacks timeline: From Paris and Brussels terror to most recent attacks in Europe.' *Express*, August 18, 2017. https://www.express.co.uk/news/world/693421/Terror-attacks-timeline-France-Brussels-Europe-ISIS-killings-Germany-dates-terrorism.

Horden, William Douglas. 'The Tao of Enlightenment.' *HuffPost Contributor*, June 4, 2011. https://www.huffpost.com/entry/the-tao-of-enlightenment_b_843432.

Irandoost, Daniele-Hadi, 'Counterintelligence: Enduring Lessons from the Cold War.' *E-International Relations*. September 18, 2017. https://www.e-ir.info/2017/09/18/counterintelligence-enduring-lessons-from-the-cold-war/.

Jackson, Marie, and Dulcie Lee. 'Sir David Amess: MP murder suspect held under Terrorism Act.' BBC. October 17, 2021. https://www.bbc.co.uk/news/uk-58943184.

Lynn III, William J. 'Defending a New Domain: The Pentagon's Cyberstrategy.' *Foreign Affairs*, September 1, 2010. https://www.foreignaffairs.com/articles/united-states/2010-09-01/defending-new-domain.

Stoddart, Kristan. 'Life through a PRISM: Data Mining, Processing Capacity and Intelligence Gathering.' *E-International Relations*. July 4, 2013. https://www.e-ir.info/2013/07/04/life-through-a-prism-data-mining-processing-capacity-and-intelligence-gathering/.

Sweet, William. 'Jeremy Bentham (1748—1832).' *Internet Encyclopaedia of Philosophy*. Accessed March 16, 2016. https:// iep.utm.edu/jeremy-bentham/

Tardi, Carla. 'What Is Moore's Law and Is It Still True?' *Investopedia*. Updated July 17, 2022. https://www.investopedia. com/terms/m/mooreslaw.asp.

West, Henry R., and Brian Duignan. 'Utilitarianism.' *Encyclopedia Britannica*. October 19, 2022. https://www.britannica.com/topic/ utilitarianism-philosophy.

REPORTS AND OTHER OFFICIAL DOCUMENTS

Cabinet Office. *Government Response to the Intelligence and Security Committee of Parliament Report on Women in the UK Intelligence Community*. Cm 9271. London: Her Majesty's Stationery Office, May 2016. https://isc.independent.gov.uk/ wp-content/uploads/2021/01/20160526_Women_in_intelli- gence_community_Government_Response.pdf.

Dawson, Joanna, and Samantha Godec. *Oversight of the intel- ligence agencies: a comparison of the "Five Eyes" nations*. House of Commons Library Briefing Paper No. 7921. London: House of Commons Library, 2017. https://researchbriefings.files.parlia- ment.uk/documents/CBP-7921/CBP-7921.pdf.

European Union Agency for Fundamental Rights. *Surveillance by intelligence services: fundamental rights safeguards and remedies in the EU*. Vol. 1. Luxembourg: Publications Office of the European Union, 2017. https://fra.europa.eu/sites/default/files/fra_uploads/ fra-2015-surveillance-intelligence-services-voi-1_en.pdf.

Home Office. *Investigatory Powers Bill: Government Response to Pre-Legislative Scrutiny*. Cm 9219. London: Her Majesty's Stationery Office, 2016. https://assets.publishing.service.gov. uk/government/uploads/system/uploads/attachment_data/

file/504298/54575_Cm_9219_PRINT.pdf.

Intelligence and Security Committee of Parliament. 'Statement by the Chairman, the Rt. Hon. Dominic Grieve QC MP.' March 17, 2017. https://isc.independent.gov.uk/news/.

Intelligence and Security Committee of Parliament. *Privacy and Security: A modern and transparent legal framework.* HC 1075. London: Her Majesty's Stationery Office, 2015. https://isc.independent.gov.uk/wp-content/uploads/2021/01/20150312_ISC_PSRptweb.pdf.

Intelligence and Security Committee of Parliament. *Report on the draft Investigatory Powers Bill.* HC 795. London: Her Majesty's Stationery Office, 2016. https://isc.independent.gov.uk/wp-content/uploads/2021/01/20160209_ISC_Rpt_IPBillweb.pdf.

Intelligence and Security Committee of Parliament. *UK Lethal Drone Strikes in Syria.* HC 1152. London: Her Majesty's Stationery Office, 2017. https://isc.independent.gov.uk/wp-content/uploads/2021/01/20170426_UK_Lethal_Drone_Strikes_in_Syria_Report.pdf.

Intelligence and Security Committee of Parliament. *Women in the UK Intelligence Community.* HC 970. London: Her Majesty's Stationery Office, 2015. https://isc.independent.gov.uk/wp-content/uploads/2021/01/20150305_ISC_Report_Women_in_the_UKIC.pdf.

Intelligence Services Act 1994. https://www.legislation.gov.uk/ukpga/1994/13/contents/enacted.

Investigatory Powers Act 2016. https://www.legislation.gov.uk/ukpga/2016/25/contents/enacted.

Justice and Security Act 2013. https://www.legislation.gov.uk/ukpga/2013/18/contents/enacted.

National Commission on Terrorist Attacks Upon the United States. *The 9/11 Commission Report*. Washington: U.S. Government Printing Office, 2004. https://www.govinfo.gov/content/pkg/GPO-911REPORT/pdf/GPO-911REPORT.pdf.

Nolan, Andrew. *Cybersecurity and Information Sharing: Legal Challenges and Solutions*. CRS Report No. R43941. Washington, DC: Congressional Research Service, 2015. https://sgp.fas.org/crs/intel/R43941.pdf.

Security Service Act 1989. https://www.legislation.gov.uk/ukpga/1989/5/enacted.

U.S. Department of Defense. 'DoD News Briefing - Secretary Rumsfeld and Gen. Myers.' February 12, 2002. https://archive.ph/20180320091111/http://archive.defense.gov/Transcripts/Transcript.aspx?TranscriptID=2636.

U.S. Marine Corps. *Counterintelligence*. MCWP 2-14. Washington, DC: Department of the Navy, 2000. https://irp.fas.org/doddir/usmc/mcwp2-14.pdf.

ACKNOWLEDGEMENTS

I would like to thank Gwendolyn Taunton for believing in this project, John Barnwell, Neil Watson, Monsignor Alan Cox, and the inspiration I continually receive from renowned activists, such as Peter Wright, David Shayler, and Julian Assange.

SOURCE NOTES

Instead of footnotes or endnotes, it was decided to place these source notes at the end of the book. Overall, this is an attempt to make these materials accessible and modernize the manner within which people can compare as well as contrast these references. A system I intend to employ in future works due to the fact these materials need to be very carefully presented to the public because of their occasionally bewildering origin and inherent complexity.

PART I

CHAPTER I

[1] David William Parry, 'Art, Espionage, and Occultism' (lecture, Yunus Emre Institute, London, October 4, 2018).

[2] Richard B. Spence, 'Secret Agent 666: Aleister Crowley and British Intelligence in America, 1914-1918,' *International Journal of Intelligence and CounterIntelligence* 13, no. 3 (2000): 259ff., https://doi.org/10.1080/08850600050140634.

[3] Tao, or 'the Way,' is 'a naturally occurring state of profound harmony with all things that manifests as the purest form of participation in life.' To this may be further added the importance of

yin and yang; both have an evident tendency to establish a dynamic system within which the whole might be greater than the elementary parts. David William Parry finds already decreed, in the last analysis, that 'even this Divine Couple point towards an even greater Truth beyond other dichotomous moral judgments. At the end of the day, this admitted, the duality of Negative and Positive is an indivisible whole.' It is no wonder therefore that, the wisdom of the ancients is such as to oblige them to apply the same principle to every case that may arise. William Douglas Horden, 'The Tao of Enlightenment,' *HuffPost Contributor*, June 4, 2011, https://www.huffpost.com/entry/the-tao-of-enlightenment_b_843432; Parry, 'Art, Espionage, and Occultism.'

4 Peter Wright and Paul Greengrass, *Spycatcher: The Candid Autobiography of a Senior Intelligence Officer* (London: Viking, 1987), 169.

5 Wright and Greengrass, *Spycatcher*, 169.

6 U.S. Marine Corps, *Counterintelligence*, MCWP 2-14 (Washington, DC: Department of the Navy, 2000), 1-7, https://irp.fas.org/doddir/usmc/mcwp2-14.pdf.

7 Daniele-Hadi Irandoost, 'Counterintelligence: Enduring Lessons from the Cold War,' *E-International Relations*, September 18, 2017, https://www.e-ir.info/2017/09/18/counterintelligence-enduring-lessons-from-the-cold-war/.

8 Eric Rosenbach and Aki J. Peritz, *Confrontation or Collaboration? Congress and the Intelligence Community* (Cambridge, MA: The Belfer Center, Harvard University, 2009), 32, https://www.belfercenter.org/sites/default/files/legacy/files/IC-book-finalasof12JUNE.pdf.

9 Rosenbach and Peritz, *Confrontation or Collaboration?*, 32.

10 Albert E. Riffice, 'Intelligence and Covert Action,' *Studies in Intelligence* 6, no. 1 (Winter 1962): 73-80.

11 Richards J. Heuer, Jr., 'Strategic Deception and Counterdeception: A Cognitive Process Approach,' *International Studies Quarterly* 25, no. 2 (June 1981): 294, https://doi.org/10.2307/2600359.

12 Wright and Greengrass, *Spycatcher*, 169.

13 Phillip Knightley, *The Second Oldest Profession: Spies and Spying in the Twentieth Century* (New York; London: W. W. Norton & Company, 1987).

[14] Christopher Andrew and David Dilks, introduction to *The Missing Dimension: Governments and Intelligence Communities in the Twentieth Century*, ed. Christopher Andrew and David Dilks (London: Palgrave Macmillan, 1984), 1.

CHAPTER II

[15] Sir David Omand and Mark Phythian make use of examples and testimonies to represent this point in 'Ethics and Intelligence: A Debate,' *International Journal of Intelligence and Counterintelligence* 26, no. 1 (2013), 38-63, doi.org/10.1080/08 850607.2012.705186; Alex J. Bellamy, 'Dirty Hands and Lesser Evils in the War on Terror,' *The British Journal of Politics and International Relations* 9, no. 3 (2007): 509-526, https://doi.org/10.1111/j.1467-856x.2006.00255.x.

[16] Samantha Newbery, 'Terrorism, Torture and Intelligence,' *International Politics* 50, no. 4 (2013): 512, DOI:10.1057/ip.2013.20.

[17] Julia Driver, 'The History of Utilitarianism,' in *The Stanford Encyclopedia of Philosophy*, ed. Edward N. Zalta and Uri Nodelman, Winter 2022 ed., http://plato.stanford.edu/entries/utilitarianism-history/.

[18] William Sweet, 'Jeremy Bentham (1748—1832),' *The Internet Encyclopedia of Philosophy*, accessed February 1, 2023, https://iep.utm.edu/jeremy-bentham/.

[19] Kent Pekel, 'The Need for Improvement: Integrity, Ethics, and the CIA,' in *Ethics of Spying: A Reader for the Intelligence Professional*, ed. Jan Goldman (Lanham, MD: Scarecrow Press, 2006), 52-65; Henry R. West and Brian Duignan, 'Utilitarianism,' *Encyclopaedia Britannica*, October 19, 2022, https://www.britannica.com/topic/utilitarianism-philosophy.

[20] Tony Pfaff and Jeffrey R. Tiel, 'The Ethics of Espionage,' *Journal of Military Ethics* 3, no. 1 (2004): 1-15, https://doi.org/10.1080/15027570310004447; The Editors of Encyclopaedia Britannica, 'Categorical Imperative,' *Encyclopedia Britannica*, February 10, 2023, http://www.britannica.com/topic/categorical-imperative.

[21] David Sussman, 'What's Wrong with Torture?,' *Philosophy &*

Public Affairs 33, no. 1 (2005): 22, https://doi.org/10.1111/j.1088-4963.2005.00023.x; Ross Bellaby, 'What's The Harm? The Ethics of Intelligence Collection,' *Intelligence and National Security* 27, no. 1 (2012): 96, https://doi.org/10.1080/02684527.2012.621600.

[22] Fritz Allhoff, 'An Ethical Defense of Torture in Interrogation,' in *Ethics of Spying: A Reader for the Intelligence Professional*, ed. Jan Goldman (Lanham, MD: Scarecrow Press, 2006), 130.

[23] Arthur S. Hulnick and David W. Mattausch, 'Ethics and Morality in U.S. Secret Intelligence,' in *Ethics of Spying: A Reader for the Intelligence Professional*, ed. Jan Goldman (Lanham, MD: Scarecrow Press, 2006), 42-44.

[24] Allhoff, 'An Ethical Defense of Torture in Interrogation,' 132-136.

[25] Christian Barry, 'A Challenge to the Reigning Theory of the Just War,' *International Affairs* 87, no. 2 (2011): 457, http://www.jstor.org/stable/20869670.

[26] Michael Quinlan, 'Just Intelligence: Prolegomena to an Ethical Theory,' *Intelligence and National Security* 22, no. 1 (2007): 8, https://doi.org/10.1080/02684520701200715.

[27] Vittorio Bufacchi and Jean Maria Arrigo, 'Torture, Terrorism and the State: A Refutation of the Ticking-Bomb Argument,' *Journal of Applied Philosophy* 23, no. 3 (2006): 360-362, http://www.jstor.org/stable/24355182.

[28] J. E. Drexel Godfrey, 'Ethics and Intelligence,' in *Ethics of Spying: A Reader for the Intelligence Professional*, ed. Jan Goldman (Lanham, MD: Scarecrow Press, 2006), 1-17.

CHAPTER III

[29] Christopher Andrew and David Dilks, introduction to *The Missing Dimension: Governments and Intelligence Communities in the Twentieth Century*, ed. Christopher Andrew and David Dilks (London: Palgrave Macmillan, 1984), 1.

[30] The brief discourse in the following volume gives an account of all the variety of interdisciplinary approaches to the study of intelligence; Peter Gill and Mark Phythian, *Intelligence in an Insecure World*, 2nd ed. (Cambridge: Polity Press, 2012), 1-9.

[31] Abram N. Shulsky and Gary J. Schmitt, *Silent Warfare: Understanding the World of Intelligence*, 3rd ed. (Washington: Potomac Books, 2002): 1.

[32] Shulsky and Schmitt, *Silent Warfare*, 2.

[33] Norbert Elias, *The Civilizing Process: Sociogenetic and Psychogenetic Investigations*, ed. Eric Dunning, Johan Goudsblom and Stephen Mennell, trans. Edmund Jephcott, rev. ed. (Oxford: Blackwell Publishers, 2000), 197ff.

[34] Elias, *The Civilizing Process*, 268ff.

[35] Andrew Linklater and Stephen Mennell, 'Norbert Elias, the Civilizing Process: Sociogenetic and Psychogenetic Investigations—An Overview and Assessment,' *History and Theory* 49, no. 3 (October 2010): 401, https://www.jstor.org/stable/40864499.

[36] Jock Haswell, *Spies and Spymasters: A Concise History of Intelligence* (London: Thames and Hudson, 1977), 21.

[37] Gill and Phythian, *Intelligence in an Insecure World*, 21.

[38] Haswell, *Spies and Spymasters*, 28-30.

[39] Andrew Linklater, 'Process sociology and international relations,' in *Norbert Elias and Figurational Research: Processual Thinking in Sociology*, ed. Norman Gabriel and Stephen Mennell (Malden, MA: Wiley-Blackwell/Sociological Review, 2011), 48-64; Andrew Linklater, *The Problem of Harm in World Politics: Theoretical Investigations* (Cambridge: Cambridge University Press, 2011).

[40] Martin Wight, *Systems of States*, ed. Hedley Bull (Leicester: Leicester University Press, 1977), 22.

[41] Martin Rudner, 'Hunters and Gatherers: The Intelligence Coalition Against Islamic Terrorism,' *International Journal of Intelligence and CounterIntelligence* 17, no. 2 (2004): 193ff., https://doi.org/10.1080/08850600490274890.

[42] Elias, *The Civilizing Process*, 235.

[43] Andrew Linklater, 'International Society and the Civilizing Process.' *Ritsumeikan International Affairs* 9 (2011): 13ff.

[44] It is worth mentioning, there is another element to 'established-outsider relations,' such as it is there seen or perceived to be in relation to the internalization of the sense of inferiority in the outsider and its endeavors to 'emulate' the established group.

I did not pursue this inquiry since there is little evidence of the feelings of non-anglophone intelligence agencies towards their anglophone counterparts. Either way, this perception of things should not be neglected or forgotten as it may entail or offer an insight into research projects for the future.

[45] Gill and Phythian, *Intelligence in an Insecure World*, 188ff.

[46] Andrew Linklater, 'Torture and Civilisation,' *International Relations* 21, no. 1 (2007): 114ff., https://doi.org/10.1177/0047117807073771.

[47] Tanja Collet, 'Civilization and civilized in post-9/11 US presidential speeches,' *Discourse & Society* 20, no. 4 (2009): 455-475, https://www.jstor.org/stable/42889273.

[48] Elias, *The Civilizing Process*, 152.

[49] R. V. Jones, *Reflections on Intelligence* (London: Heinemann, 1989), 52.

CHAPTER IV

[50] Carla Tardi, 'What Is Moore's Law and Is It Still True?,' *Investopedia*, updated July 17, 2022, https://www.investopedia.com/terms/m/mooreslaw.asp.

[51] E. Gabriella Coleman, *Coding Freedom: The Ethics and Aesthetics of Hacking* (Princeton; Oxford: Princeton University Press, 2013), 207, https://doi.org/10.2307/j.ctt1r2gbj.

[52] James Curran, Natalie Fenton and Des Freedman, *Misunderstanding the Internet* (London: Routledge, 2012), 9ff.

[53] M. Aaron Dennis, 'Cybercrime,' *Encyclopedia Britannica*, December 15, 2022, https://www.britannica.com/topic/cybercrime.

[54] Jason Whittaker, *The Cyberspace Handbook* (London; New York: Routledge, 2003), 284.

[55] Kristan Stoddart, 'Life through a PRISM: Data Mining, Processing Capacity and Intelligence Gathering,' *E-International Relations*, July 4, 2013, https://www.e-ir.info/2013/07/04/life-through-a-prism-data-mining-processing-capacity-and-intelligence-gathering/.

[56] As a case in point, European Union Agency for Fundamental Rights, *Surveillance by intelligence services: fundamental rights safeguards and remedies in the EU*, vol. 1 (Luxembourg: Publications Office of the European Union, 2017), https://fra.europa.eu/sites/default/files/fra_uploads/fra-2015-surveillance-intelligence-services-voi-1_en.pdf.

[57] Alasdair Roberts, 'WikiLeaks: the illusion of transparency,' *International Review of Administrative Sciences* 78, no. 1 (2012): 116ff., https://doi.org/10.1177/0020852311429428.

[58] Kristan Stoddart, 'Live Free or Die Hard: U.S.-UK Cybersecurity Policies,' *Political Science Quarterly* 131, nc. 4 (Winter 2016): 826, https://doi.org/10.1002/polq.12535.

[59] William J. Lynn III, 'Defending a New Domain: The Pentagon's Cyberstrategy,' *Foreign Affairs*, September 1, 2010, https://www.foreignaffairs.com/articles/united-states/2010-09-01/defending-new-domain.

[60] Yoram Dinstein, 'The Principle of Distinction and Cyber War in International Armed Conflicts,' *Journal of Conflict and Security Law* 17, no. 2 (Summer 2012): 268, https://doi.org/10.1093/jcsl/krs015.

[61] Randall R. Dipert, 'The Ethics of Cyberwarfare,' *Journal of Military Ethics* 9, no. 4 (2010): 405f., https://doi.org/10.1080/150 27570.2010.536404.

[62] Nancy E. Marion, 'The Council of Europe's Cyber Crime Treaty: An exercise in Symbolic Legislation,' *International Journal of Cyber Criminology* 4, no. 1/2 (Jan-Dec 2010): 702f., https://www.cybercrimejournal.com/pdf/marion2010ijcc.pdf.

[63] This classification is derived from Thomas Rid's exposition that 'cyberwar' does not really exist; that, broadly speaking, state-to-state cyber incidents are dividable into three functions only: espionage, sabotage, and subversion (none of which on their own, he argues, can materialize as war in the full extent of the word). Though this chapter does not agree with Rid's definition of cyberwar, it follows his categorization of cyber incidents between states in a slightly modified form, by putting sabotage and subversion in one category as active measures (commonly called covert action), the other as the passive activity of gathering secret information. This approach is chosen merely because it facilitates a theoretical discussion of the subject. Thomas Rid, 'Cyber War Will Not Take Place,' *Journal of Strategic Studies* 35,

no. 1 (2012): 7ff., https://doi.org/10.1080/01402390.2011.608939.

[64] Richard A. Clarke, 'Cyberwar in 2013,' filmed December 8, 2012 in New York City, The Economist's World in 2013 Festival, 21:27, https://www.youtube.com/watch?v=6_ek8mugOUc.

[65] Richard A. Clarke and Robert K. Knake, *Cyber War: The Next Threat to National Security and What to Do About It* (New York: HarperCollins Publishers, 2010), 160ff.

[66] Andrew Nolan, *Cybersecurity and Information Sharing: Legal Challenges and Solutions*, CRS Report No. R43941 (Washington, DC: Congressional Research Service, 2015), https://sgp.fas.org/crs/intel/R43941.pdf.

PART II

INTRODUCTORY WORDS AND PLAN OF WORK

[67] Marie Jackson and Dulcie Lee, 'Sir David Amess: MP murder suspect held under Terrorism Act,' BBC, October 17, 2021, https://www.bbc.co.uk/news/uk-58943184; Alice Foster, 'Terror attacks timeline: From Paris and Brussels terror to most recent attacks in Europe,' *Express*, August 10, 2017, https://www.express.co.uk/news/world/693421/Terror-attacks-timeline-France-Brussels-Europe-ISIS-killings-Germany-dates-terrorism.

[68] Richard J. Aldrich, 'Beyond the Vigilant State: Globalisation and Intelligence,' *Review of International Studies* 35, no. 4 (2009): 889ff., http://www.jstor.org/stable/40588091.

[69] The 9/11 Commission, for instance, played a key role in these debates as the formal inquiry that investigated the causes behind the 9/11 intelligence failure; National Commission on Terrorist Attacks Upon the United States, *The 9/11 Commission Report* (Washington: U.S. Government Printing Office, 2004), https://www.govinfo.gov/content/pkg/GPO-911REPORT/pdf/GPO-911REPORT.pdf.

[70] Oversight may be defined in two ways: 'supervision' (watchful care) or 'failure to notice or consider.' Hereafter, oversight is

defined as the former. Mark M. Lowenthal, *Intelligence: From Secrets to Policy*, 7th ed. (Los Angeles: CQ Press, 2016), 304.

[71] Jack Caravelli, 'Lessons from the Iranian case and the changing face of American intelligence,' in *Intelligence and Human Rights in the Era of Global Terrorism*, ed. Steve Tsang (Westport, CT; London: Praeger Security International, 2007), 37f.

[72] Gregory F. Treverton, 'Addressing "Complexities" in Homeland Security,' in *The Oxford Handbook of National Security Intelligence*, ed. Loch K. Johnson (Oxford: Oxford University Press, 2010), 344.

[73] David Kahn, 'An historical theory of intelligence,' *Intelligence and National Security* 16, no. 3 (2001): 79-80, https://doi.org/10.1080/02684520412331306220.

[74] U.S. Department of Defense, 'DoD News Briefing - Secretary Rumsfeld and Gen. Myers,' February 12, 2002, https://archive.ph/20180320091111/http://archive.defense.gov/Transcripts/Transcript.aspx?TranscriptID=2636.

[75] This view is broadly based on the 'realist' approach to intelligence. Realists hold that national interest (*raison d'état*) is the highest moral principle; Toni Erskine, "As Rays of Light to the Human Soul?' Moral Agents and Intelligence Gathering,' *Intelligence and National Security* 19, no. 2 (2004): 364, https://doi.org/10.1080/0268452042000302047.

[76] This is the view propounded by deontologists. As a deontologist, Immanuel Kant, for instance, regarded espionage as 'intrinsically despicable;' Michael Herman, 'Ethics and Intelligence after September 2001,' *Intelligence and National Security* 19, no. 2 (2004): 342, https://doi.org/10.1080/0268452042000302038.

[77] Peter Gill and Mark Phythian, *Intelligence in an Insecure World*, 2nd ed. (Cambridge: Polity, 2012), 170.

[78] David Omand, 'Can we have the Pleasure of the Grin without Seeing the Cat? Must the Effectiveness of Secret Agencies Inevitably Fade on Exposure to the Light?,' *Intelligence and National Security* 23, no. 5 (2008): 594-595, https://doi.org/10.1080/02684520802449476.

[79] Michael Quinlan, 'Just intelligence: Prolegomena to an ethical theory,' *Intelligence and National Security* 22, no. 1 (2007): 7ff. https://doi.org/10.1080/02684520701200715.

[80] Generally speaking, other oversight mechanisms

complementing the three bodies originate from Parliament (through debates, etcetera), the larger society (NGOs and pressure groups) and international institutions (such as the European Council). Unlike the ISC, Commissioners and Tribunal, these do not have the same level of interaction with the agencies, both in terms of access to secret information and continuity of contact.

[81] Hugh Bochel and Andrew Defty, 'Parliamentary Oversight of Intelligence Agencies: Lessons from Westminster,' in *Security in a Small Nation: Scotland, Democracy, Politics*, ed. Andrew W. Neal (Cambridge, UK: Open Book Publishers, 2017), 103-124, http://www.jstor.org/stable/j.ctt1sq5v42.9.

[82] Sources that usually contribute to the study of intelligence, in the first place, include memoirs, whistleblowing exposés, scholarly analyses and government reports; Glenn P. Hastedt, 'Controlling Intelligence: Defining the Problem,' in *Controlling Intelligence*, ed. Glenn P. Hastedt (London: Frank Cass, 1991), 5.

[83] Len Scott and Peter Jackson, 'Journeys in Shadows: Introduction,' in *Understanding Intelligence in the Twenty-First Century: Journeys in Shadows*, ed. Len Scott and Peter Jackson (London; New York: Routledge, 2004), 7.

CHAPTER V

[84] Peter Gill, "'A Formidable Power to Cause Trouble for the Government?" Intelligence Oversight and the Creation of the UK Intelligence and Security Committee,' in *Learning from the Secret Past: Cases in British Intelligence History*, ed. Robert Dover and Michael S. Goodman (Washington, DC: Georgetown University Press, 2011), 43-44.

[85] Christopher Andrew, *The Defence of the Realm: The Authorized History of MI5* (London: Penguin Books, 2010), 754ff.

[86] Marina Caparini, 'Controlling and Overseeing Intelligence Services in Democratic States,' in *Democratic Control of Intelligence Services: Containing Rogue Elephants*, ed. Hans Born and Marina Caparini (Hampshire: Ashgate, 2007), 10.

[87] Philip H. J. Davies, 'Britain's Machinery of Intelligence Accountability: Realistic Oversight in the Absence of Moral Panic,' in *Democratic Oversight of Intelligence Services*, ed. Daniel

Baldino (Leichhardt, NSW: Federation Press, 2010), 140ff.

[88] Davies, 'Britain's Machinery of Intelligence Accountability,' 140-141.

[89] Thomas P. Carroll, 'The Case Against Intelligence Openness,' *International Journal of Intelligence and CounterIntelligence* 14, no. 4 (2001): 561ff., DOI: 10.1080/08850600152617164; Abram N. Shulsky and Gary J. Schmitt, *Silent Warfare: Understanding the World of Intelligence*, 3rd ed. (Washington: Potomac Books, 2002): 144ff.

[90] Peter Gill and Mark Phythian, *Intelligence in an Insecure World*, 2nd ed. (Cambridge: Polity Press, 2012), 181.

[91] R. V. Jones, *Reflections on Intelligence* (London: Mandarin, 1990), 54.

[92] Daniel Baldino, 'Introduction: Watching the Watchmen,' in *Democratic Oversight of Intelligence Services*, ed. Daniel Baldino (Leichhardt, NSW: Federation Press, 2010), 9.

[93] Christopher Andrew, *The Defence of the Realm: The Authorized History of MI5* (London: Penguin Books, 2010), 753.

[94] Andrew Defty, 'Recent events at the Intelligence and Security Committee make it increasingly difficult to justify the current arrangements for scrutinising the security services,' *Democratic Audit UK* (blog), May 30, 2014, https://www.democraticaudit. com/2014/05/30/recent-events-at-the-intelligence-and-securi- ty-committee-make-it-increasingly-difficult-to-justify-the-cur- rent-arrangements-for-scrutinising-the-security-services/.

[95] Shulsky and Schmitt, *Silent Warfare*, 146.

[96] Claudia Hillebrand, 'Intelligence Oversight and Accountability,' in *Routledge Companion to Intelligence Studies*, ed. Robert Dover Michael S. Goodman and Claudia Hillebrand (London; New York: Routledge, 2017), 307.

[97] Reg Whitaker, *The End of Privacy: How Total Surveillance is Becoming a Reality* (New York: The New Press, 1999), 2f.; Mark M. Lowenthal, *Intelligence: From Secrets to Policy*, 7th ed. (Los Angeles: CQ Press, 2017), 303.

[98] Julian Richards, *The Art and Science of Intelligence Analysis* (Oxford: Oxford University Press, 2010), 87.

[99] Or Arthur Honig and Sarah Zimskind, 'The Spy Machine and the Ballot Box: Examining Democracy's Intelligence Advantage,' *International Journal of Intelligence and CounterIntelligence* 30,

no. 3 (2017): 437, https://doi.org/10.1080/08850607.2017.1263524.

[100] Jones, *Reflections on Intelligence*, 55.

[101] Richard L. Russell, 'Competitive Analysis: Techniques for Better Gauging Enemy Political Intentions and Military Capabilities,' in *The Oxford Handbook of National Security Intelligence*, ed. Loch K. Johnson (Oxford: Oxford University Press, 2010), 375-388; John N. L. Morrison, 'Political Supervision of Intelligence Services in the United Kingdom,' in *Intelligence and Human Rights in the Era of Global Terrorism*, ed. Steve Tsang (Westport, CT; London: Praeger Security International, 2007), 51; Uri Bar-Joseph and Rose McDermott, 'The Intelligence Analysis Crisis,' in *The Oxford Handbook of National Security Intelligence*, ed. Loch K. Johnson (Oxford: Oxford University Press, 2010), 359ff.

[102] Richard J. Aldrich, 'Global Intelligence Co-operation versus Accountability: New Facets to an Old Problem,' *Intelligence and National Security* 24, no. 1 (2009): 30, https://doi.org/10.1080/02684520902756812.

[103] Jones, *Reflections on Intelligence*, 53.

[104] Steve Tsang, 'Stopping Global Terrorism and Protecting Rights,' in *Intelligence and Human Rights in the Era of Global Terrorism*, ed. Steve Tsang (Westport, CT; London: Praeger Security International, 2007), 1-14.

[105] Peter Gill, 'Intelligence, Threat, Risk and the Challenge of Oversight,' *Intelligence and National Security* 27, no. 2 (2012): 221, https://doi.org/10.1080/02684527.2012.661643.

[106] David Omand, 'Can we have the Pleasure of the Grin without Seeing the Cat? Must the Effectiveness of Secret Agencies Inevitably Fade on Exposure to the Light?,' *Intelligence and National Security* 23, no. 5 (2008): 606, https://doi.org/10.1080/02684520802449476.

CHAPTER VI

[107] From March 2015 to May 2017, the Committee has published various reports. These include *Women in the UK Intelligence Community* (March 2015); *Privacy and Security: A modern and transparent legal framework* (March 2015); *Report on the draft*

Investigatory Powers Bill (February 2016); *Annual Report 2015-2016* (July 2016); and *UK Drone Strikes in Syria* (April 2017).

[108] Peter Gill, 'Evaluating intelligence oversight committees: The UK Intelligence and Security Committee and the 'war on terror," *Intelligence and National Security* 22, no. 1 (2007): 21ff, https://doi.org/10.1080/02684520701200756.

[109] Intelligence and Security Committee of Parliament, *Privacy and Security: A modern and transparent legal framework*, HC 1075 (London: Her Majesty's Stationery Office, 2015), https://isc.independent.gov.uk/wp-content/uploads/2021/01/20150312_ISC_PSRptweb.pdf.

[110] The report specifically detailed what the following are and how they are conducted by the agencies: targeted interception of communications; bulk interception of communications; accessing communications data; bulk personal datasets; 'intrusive surveillance' (conducted inside a person's home, hotel room, car or other private place); 'directed surveillance' (in a public place); interfering with property (personal possessions or specific premises); information technology operations – gaining (what would otherwise be unauthorized) access to, or interfering with, computing devices; interfering with wireless telegraphy (radio signals); and covert human intelligence sources, otherwise known as agents.

[111] The Committee's own definition of a 'bearer' is most succinct: 'Internet communications are primarily carried over international [fiber] optic cables. Each cable may carry several 'bearers' which can carry up to 10 gigabits of data per second.'

[112] Julian Borger, and Patrick Wintour and Jessica Elgot, 'Trump stands by unsubstantiated claim that British intelligence spied on him,' *The Guardian*, March 17, 2017, https://www.theguardian.com/us-news/2017/mar/17/white-house-will-not-be-repeat-claims-gchq-spied-trump-.

CHAPTER VII

[113] Amy B. Zegart, *Eyes on Spies: Congress and the United States Intelligence Community* (Stanford, Calif.: Hoover Institution Press, 2011), 20.

[114] 'UK spy watchdog "taken in" by security agencies - MP,' BBC, February 27, 2015, https://www.bbc.co.uk/news/election-2015-31665312.

[115] Andrew Defty, 'General Election 2017: The Unwelcome Impact on the Work of the Intelligence and Security Committee,' *RUSI Commentary* (blog), RUSI, May 10, 2017, https://rusi.org/explore-our-research/publications/commentary/general-election-2017-unwelcome-impact-work-intelligence-and-security-committee.

[116] Zegart, *Eyes on Spies*, 89.

[117] Peter Gill, *Policing Politics: Security Intelligence and the Liberal Democratic State* (London: Frank Cass, 1994), 35.

[118] Rhodri Jeffreys-Jones, preface to *Intelligence Studies in Britain and the US: Historiography since 1945*, ed. Christopher R. Moran and Christopher J. Murphy (Edinburgh: Edinburgh University Press, 2013), xvi.

[119] Loch K. Johnson, 'Intelligence Oversight in the United States,' in *Intelligence and Human Rights in the Era of Global Terrorism*, ed. Steve Tsang (Westport, CT; London: Praeger Security International, 2007), 62.

[120] Johnson, 'Intelligence Oversight in the United States,' 62.

[121] Aurelius, *Meditations*, 7.18

APPENDIX

[122] A few social liberals include L. T. Hobhouse, J. A. Hobson and T. H. Green, among others.

AFTERWORD

[123] This passage can be translated as: 'from the very center of a fountain of delights arises something bitter that chokes us in our prime.'